POP YOUR BUBBLES

SALONI S JAIN

FANATIXX PUBLICATION

FanatiXx® Publication

AM/56, Basanti Colony, Rourkela 769012, Odisha

ISO 9001:2015 Certified

© Copyright, 2023 Saloni S Jain

All rights reserved. No part of this book may be reproduced, stored in a retrieval system, or transmitted, in any form by any means, electronic, mechanical, magnetic, optical, chemical, manual, photocopying, recording, or otherwise, without the prior written consent of the author.

By: Saloni S Jain

ISBN: 9789356056381

Book: Pop Your Bubbles

Price: INR 299/-

Cover By: Noorleen Kaur Bhatia

Book Formatting by Hemant Bansal

Printing By: BooksClub.in

The opinions/ contents expressed in this book are the sole of the author and do not represent the opinions/ stands/ thoughts of FanatiXx® or any of its associates and affiliations.

DISCLAIMER

All rights reserved. This book may not be reproduced in whole or in part, or transmitted in any form, without written permission from the publisher, nor may any part of this book be reproduced, stored in a retrieval system, or transmitted in any form or by any means electronic, mechanical, photocopying, microfilming, and recording without written permission from the publisher.

Author assures that all content is original, and he/she has full rights to publish and distribute the same. In any case of plagiarism, the publisher is not liable.

FOREWORD

'**Pop Your Bubbles**' is a book that will pop all the bubbles of misconceptions and fears from our lives. It tries to show you the real mirror of this complex diversified world. As you read, you will find real-life instances which will help you chase yourself, and keep you motivated. Inspiring quotes in the chapters are just like a cherry on the cake! The book itself, being a plethora of experiences, helps a person relate well to the execution of real-life chores.

Along with this, it will also force your attentiveness to comprehend all the aspects described in it.

Different topics have been made into different chapters for better grasping! Many phrases have been used to glorify the content. This is a book that will develop you with confidence, kindness, wisdom, and a completely new perspective to understand and chase life.

*- **Harsh M. Chheda (HMCKBC)** - Author of "The Mindful Peace"*

This book is really needed in this age as it's straight to the point in helping you understand yourself. Every chapter has its own perception and will be absorbed by anyone who reads relating to their own experiences. Saloni is highly aware and has put good efforts to sort the basics of being a human. Also, the **"Actionable Insights"** on every chapter helps in taking personalized steps for betterment. Special mention to the last chapter which is about "How to know yourself" aces the value add to our lives.

*- **Benjamin Ekorhi (@the.wholistic.coach)** – Relationship & Life Coach*

---

*- Thank you **Harsh & Benjamin** for diligently reading my book and providing your valuable feedback for my readers.*

ABOUT THE AUTHOR

Meet Saloni S Jain, a 24-year-old entrepreneur, spiritual seeker, software developer and now an author with this debut book. The author is on a journey to discover herself while blending creativity and innovation. This inspiring individual explores spirituality for personal and professional growth, expressing their insights through profound poetry. As an entrepreneur, Saloni S Jain is committed to making a positive impact by weaving narratives of change through both words and code.

Since 9th grade, writing has been Saloni's companion, shaping them into an optimistic soul. With a blog on Instagram, *@authorsaloni*, Saloni engages with the readers with her writings, offering exactly what they need and fostering meaningful interactions. It blossomed into a passionate pursuit, providing a platform for self-expression and connection. In addition to their pursuits, Saloni has played a role as a guiding light for friends, helping them build self-awareness and facilitating a smoother path in their lives.

INTRODUCTION

"The first step towards change is awareness. The second step is acceptance." - Nathaniel Branden

Self-awareness/Self-help... which occurs first? Self-awareness should occur before self-help in my opinion because only if you are aware of your mistakes, you can help yourself, change. In the intricate dance of self-improvement, the spotlight first falls on self-awareness as an essential precursor to meaningful change. Much like our instinctive recoil when we touch a hot vessel, acknowledging our mistakes (touching hot vessel) and becoming aware of the same, becomes the catalyst for transformation. It's a conscious awareness that certain actions are akin to touching a hot surface which hurts, and we instinctively yearn for a shift. Awareness demands being in the present and observing ourselves keenly without any internal biases. Awareness is a philosophical notion which says, ***"JUST BE"***. Yet, in the vast landscape of personal growth, millions of unnoticed errors persist. Once we illuminate these blind spots with awareness and focus, a conscious choice to evolve/change emerges. This book becomes a trusted ally in this expedition where it sows the seed of awareness inside you about yourself. This book will help you watch yourself from a new perspective guiding you through introspective exercises and illuminating narratives—a compass pointing towards the enriched and fulfilling life that unfolds when self-awareness precedes the journey of self-improvement.

ACKNOWLEDGEMENT

Gratitude to all the individuals in my life who've colored my world and the experiences that shaped my journey – especially,

My lovable parents – B Sanjay Kumar & Sangeetha S Jain,

My siblings aka partners in crime – Simoni S Jain & Dhavaj S Jain

And

All my close friends.

Your presence and impact are the essence of my story.

CONTENT

Experience-Tinted Lenses – Judgements	1
Beyond The Clock – What is Time?	5
Decisions And Choices	8
Investing In Growth Amidst Pains	11
The Positivity Paradox	15
Dance Of Endings And Beginnings	18
The Intricate Web Of Impressions And Judgments	22
Unveiling The Authentic Soul	26
Stereotypes In The Midst Of Diversity	30
The Loneliness-Boredom Tango	35
From Idols To Realities	40
Crafting Responses Beyond Personality Labels	43
Navigating Life's Three Perspectives	46
Navigating The Bond Between Body And Soul	50
Insights From Water, Time, And Babies	55
Choices, Desires, And True Satisfaction	59
Embracing Emotions	63
Attachment's Embrace And Detachment's Freedom	68
Chasing Dreams, Embracing Wonder	74
The Magic Of Perception	77
Navigating The Winds Of Change	81

Finding Balance Amidst The Chaos	85
The Wisdom Of Bruises And Bumps	88
Learning From Emotional Lessons	93
Guiding Lights On The Path To Authenticity	97
From Patterns To Possibilities	100
The Power Of Positive Expectations In Relationships	109
Emotional Kaleidoscope: A Journey Beyond Labels	114
Finding Harmony In Every Moment	117
The Art Of Living Fully	120
Painting A Journey Free From Comparisons	123
How Childhood Shapes Our Notion Of Home	127
Discovering Poetry In Life's Everyday Moments	131
The Power Of Unwrapping The Present	134
Messages to "Pop Your Bubbles" (Must Read)	**137**
Thought Provoking Thoughts	171
How To Know Self?	176
Why Don't Self-Help Books Work Nowadays?	183

Saloni S Jain

x

1.

SEEING LIFE THROUGH EXPERIENCE-TINTED LENSES

People see from what they know.

People judge from what they know.

People look from the window of their eyes.

People's prejudice is from their experience,

And one of those "people" is you as well.

<u>**Quote says:**</u>

Your life and its quality depends on what you experience, how you take and see it. You tend to judge the people based what you know and how you understand them, not how or what they are. Either you see them how you want them to be, or you see them from your experiences. You do not really see or observe.

Life's like a rollercoaster, isn't it? You have all ridden through various phases – the highs and lows, the ups and downs, the cheers and tears, and the times you've felt both on top of the world and stuck in a rut. Those moments of feeling like a superhero when you want to crawl under a blanket and hide, sound familiar? From the solitude of loneliness to the warmth of friendship, from the sense of worthiness to the shadow of self-doubt, your narrative comprises an array of shades, affirmation and denial, affection, and animosity. I got to admit, we all share a beautiful and messy story.

Amidst this ever-changing mural of existence, one unshakable truth persists: CHANGE is your constant companion. It is the untiring thread that weaves the very fabric of your lives. Change brings about experiences in every individual and from there arises the unique humans who drives every thought subjectively.

Imagine, a closet filled with experiences – some timeless classics, others daring experiments. Each experience weaves a stitch into the fabric of your being. Just like stitches unite fabric pieces, your experiences hold us together. They are the glue that prevents us from unraveling, much like a kitten's playful tug at a ball of yarn. These experiences are your story's treasures, your badges of honor. Two people can barely be similar but will never be the same. Remember, are all bundles of experiences, each holding memories, emotions, and enlightening moments. Even identical twins, with their similar DNA, possess chests of experiences as distinct as snowflakes. Born with identical limbs, yet only experience tames their uniqueness.

Think of yourself as a moviegoer, donning unique spectacles – not of glass, but of your experiences. These special specs tinge your view towards life. Everything is filtered through these lenses, as you watch the roles in the film. It is like watching a comedy movie through a self-customized sci-fi lens, reality becomes a thrilling kaleidoscope. In essence, everyone judges and understands from their own experiences and beliefs.

Let me talk about a memorable event – a dance fusion from my life. On stage, we danced to our rhythm, each adding their twist to the signature-step, and I observed that we all were doing a signature step partially different in comparison with the movie step, but we were all uniform. An orchestra of individualism emerged, creating a harmonious symphony of uniqueness. The audience, too, donned their experience specs. Some hummed along to the familiar tune, some nitpicked on us for the wrong step in comparison with the original, some took it as a creative step and others were puzzled over the melody. This underscores how experiences lend distinctive hues and judgements to our perceptions.

Now, a tale of Priya, a millennium kid, and her orthodox parents. They grew up in an era where degrees were as rare as unicorn sightings. So, naturally, they urged Priya to pursue a degree, a ticket to their unfulfilled dreams. But degrees today can feel like QR codes – promising access to hidden treasure yet often leading to elusive rewards. Priya's parents hand her a map of their uncharted territory, hoping she will uncover gems they never did. There is nothing to benefit out of superimposing our experiences unto others.

You are the protagonist in your tale and supporting actor in others. As directors, actors, and critics, you scatter judgments like confetti. But seeking approval is not your role. Fearing judgment traps you in a vicious cycle. Instead, focus on your story; you are the hero, not an auditionee. As Ralph Waldo Emerson said, **"To be yourself in a world that is constantly trying to make you something else is the greatest accomplishment."**

Speaking of judgment, let me talk about that imaginary arena where you often find yourself in the fear of being judged. You are guilty of stepping into that ring, wondering what others will think of you. But here is the deal: that is a one-way ticket to your self-doubt land. Imagine pouring all your energy into worrying about someone's opinion – it is like tossing your time into a black hole. Instead, focus on being the star of your own show. Embrace those experiences, wear those spectacles with pride, and dance to the rhythm of your own authentic self.

Life is a treasure map with no predefined path. You are the explorer of your narrative, not the inheritor of another's journey. Forge your path, guided by your experiential compass. Let your stories shape you, your actions, your view of the world. As the winds of change blow, steer your ship towards the 'X' on your unique map.

Actionable Insights: Next time you catch yourself worrying about judgment, pause. Take a breath. Remember those experience-tinted spectacles. Embrace the uniqueness of your journey and remind yourself that just as you cannot fully step into someone else's shoes, they cannot step into yours either. It is time to give that fear of judgment a high-five and move on. You are the conductor. Own it, wear those spectacles, and enjoy the show!

Hmmm... If you stop the fear of being judged, then won't you stop upskilling for a singing performance and just be legit raw? Won't you tend show up late for an important meeting? The key is to find a balance but that is a chat for some other day, *Think!* *Because it is all interconnected.*

BEYOND THE CLOCK: ANALOGIES, ATTITUDES, AND CHERISHED MOMENTS

Is it that you do not have time or time was never ours,' ever?

Is it that time was always yours' and you never learnt to value it the right way.

Is it that time is valuable or is it that time is trash and inexpensive.

Quote Says:

Time is always around, ticking and has no value as such. You add value to it. To a person who has goals and has priorities in life, time is valuable. To him time is precious as he adds value to his time. To the rest, perhaps time exists like the wall paintings and the photo frames in your homes, so that you know it is present, it just adds spice or adds to organize their day.

Time, a Friend to All and None: Just as "A friend to all is a friend to none," time stands as a universal companion. It belongs to everyone, yet to no one exclusively. Time bridges humanity, unyielding in its consistency.

The Illusion of Time: You've woven a spell of illusion around time, crafting clocks and watches to contain its vastness. These manufactured contraptions give us the illusion of control over time, yet it remains omnipresent, ticking universally.

Mirage of Moments: Time, like a desert mirage, teases us with promises of endless moments. The more you strive to grasp it, the more it eludes your hold. Those precious moments are fleeting, slipping through your fingers like grains of sand.

Meet Rustin, Rocky, and Pranay, each navigating time's currents uniquely. Rustin, without defined goals does not add value to his time, treats it as an afterthought, while Rocky invests in aspirations & wants to win without cherishing time's intrinsic value. Pranay seamlessly intertwines his ambitions with time's worth. He values his goals and to achieve them, he values time in return, becoming a sage of time management.

Rocky selfishly values only his own time and Pranay extends respect to others time by not keeping others on waits or delays. Pranay realizes that as he has priorities in his life, the rest of the world has it too. Attitudes towards time reveal Pranay's dependability, self-assuredness, and organization, standing in contrast to Rocky's self-centeredness and Rustin's apathy. If you respect your time, it will automatically lead you to respect others time and when you respect and add value to time, time grows positively for you.

Your treatment of time resonates in your respect for others time. Pranay's regard for his own time naturally blooms into respect for others. The reverse is often false – disregard for one's time often leads to neglect of others. This serves as a reminder that time is a shared treasure, bridging humanity. That is why punctuality is an important skill to be learnt.

Actionable Insights:

To truly fathom and value time, initiate a "Time Journal." Dedicate moments daily to reflect on time's role in your life. By acknowledging moments of growth, connection, and value, your appreciation for time will organically extend to the broader world.

Hmmm.... But how would life exist without time? The absence of time reverberates as an impossibility, underlining its omnipresence. *Think! Because it is all interconnected.*

DECISIONS AND CHOICES: NAVIGATING LIFE'S MENU WITH A WINK AND A NOD

Choices are made only if the options are ours,

Decision is about the options given to us.

Not always it is about a Choice.

Not always it is about a decision.

<u>Quote says:</u>

Life gives us choices to choose & options to decide but you do not realize that these are poles apart. Options & choices are like chalk and cheese. You do not know how to know when you tend to choose or decide.

Pop Your Bubbles

Picture this: You're at a buffet, and the Universe is the chef whipping up various dishes. On one side, you have a tray of options, each dish promising a different flavor of experience. Here both choices and decisions will keep you caught up and you will walk through and understand how.

Let us talk choices. **Choices are those moments when life offers you options that align perfectly with your interests.** It is like the Universe saying, "Hey, what tickles your fancy today?" You are the ultimate food critic, selecting the options that make your taste buds dance a jig. Think of minor life changes as those little appetizers you choose just because they look darn good on the plate. As Mark Twain once quipped, **"The choice between right and wrong is easy, but the choice between two goods is harder."** It is like collection of all your favorite chocolates and you picking one, isn't it harder? So, go ahead, choose your goodies wisely because while you make a choice of 1 in a 100, you are not making a choice of the for ninety-nine.

But then, the universe throws in a plot twist. Let us talk about decisions which are opposites of choices. Decisions are like when you are faced with a buffet, and some dishes look appetizing while others are not of your taste, and you are expected to pick from the non-appetizing ones. Decisions are made between the given options irrespective of your interests. These decisions are not always easy; they are the hearty main courses of life, the ones that asks you to sacrifice before making it happen.

Yet, here is the kicker: Sometimes, it is more of an improv show where you are handed a role for which you did not audition. That is when decision swoops in, wearing a superhero cape and asking, "Ready for this challenge?" **Decision is like the cosmic middleman between what you want and what life serves up.** It is your way of saying, "Okay, Universe, let's see what you got!"

Think of efforts and consistency as your cosmic currency. It is like filling up the gas tank of the Universe's race car. When you go all in, revving up for a high-speed chase, the Universe responds with a thunderous engine roar. But if you decide to take a leisurely Sunday drive, the Universe will join you for a casual cruise. It is like dancing with the Universe, where your moves set the rhythm of the response.

Do you know that saying, **"Ask and you shall receive"**? It is like wanting an apple and poof, there it is, right in your hand. Life is peppered with these "apple" moments—ripe opportunities ready to be plucked. But here is the kicker: most of us navigate this buffet called life like you are at a salad bar with no glasses on, feeling blind. You end up with a plate full of wilted lettuce and a longing for more. So, here is a nugget of wisdom: pause, ponder, and pick. Life serves the options, but you are the savvy diner choosing the culinary masterpiece.

Actionable Insights: Take a daily dose of reflection. Think about a recent choice or decision – was it a zesty choice or a hearty decision? With each moment of reflection, you are fine-tuning your cosmic palate and ensuring that the Universe's drive-thru always gets your order right. After all, life's a smorgasbord; why not feast well? Enjoy the comedic symphony of life, where you are the conductor, and every choice and decision are a note in your melody.

If you don't get better at making choices and decisions, won't it all impact your life? Your current situation is because of the choices you made. *Think! Because it is all interconnected.*

LIFE'S COSMIC BARTER: INVESTING IN GROWTH AMIDST PAINS

Yes, No pain, no gain,

But make sure the pain is worth the gain,

And the gain is worth the pain.

Because bad days define your pain,

Good days speak about your pains.

<u>**Quote says:**</u>

The quality of your life is all dependent on the pain you deal with and the way you channel the pain. A few take you nowhere and the rest do wonders, turning pain into art.

Life, my friend, is a *falooda* of challenges—stress, sweat, persistence, and a sprinkle of discomfort. Imagine pain as that unexpected guest crashing every party, whether you are chasing dreams or wandering aimlessly through life's maze. But hold on, you cannot just kick back and expect the Universe to toss confetti at your feet. Nope, it is time to roll up those sleeves and join the dance.

Envision this: You are in the cosmic kitchen, concocting success. The recipe? A dash of effort, a pinch of consistency, and yes, a smidge of discomfort. I know, pain is not the spice you would choose, but trust me, it is the secret ingredient that turns ordinary dishes into extraordinary feasts. Once you have whipped up that mixture, weigh it against your desired results. Is it a masterpiece in the making, or a mere experiment destined for the compost bin?

Pain occurs when you resist some kind of force unto you. Hold up, remember **Newton's third law, "Every force has an equal and opposite reaction."** It is like an ancient sage's wisdom echoing through time. The more you resist, the tighter pain clings. The less you resist, the less excruciating it is bound to feel. You all know that a physical force in opposite direction causes friction and similarly is friction leading to pain.

The Vulnerable "**Ouch**" Zone is a state when you are most fearful wrapped in vulnerability. Ever noticed how a panicked or fearful shopper grabs everything in sight? **Fear is the ruler here; it drives you into finding all escapes in any form asap.** When pain strikes, fear is like a neon sign screaming, "Buy this, it'll heal you!" Doctors are not selling potions or syrups, but they have remedies for your worries. Fear, my friend, turns you into seekers of solutions, even if they are not the best ones.

Let us talk marketing—the slick cousin of fear. The whole marketing industry is based on creating fear. Don't they spot the pain or problems and create terror out of it - ever felt the FOMO fever from an ad? They practically whisper, "Buy now or regret forever." So that you sell yourselves to their product out of Fear Of Missing Out. When you do not pay for a product that you use, you are their product. you are money to them, they sold you as a whole, just when you were in pain and fear. Be very watchful while you are in pain. People might devastate you if you allow them to.

Here is the amazing strategy to conquer pain: **Do not fight it, surrender.** Picture pain as that dance partner leading the steps. The more you resist, the more it trips you up. So, slow dance with it, embrace it, and take it for a spin. Your ego might want to dodge pain like it is lava, but sometimes, my friend, you must wave through that molten mess to find clarity. You need to introspect the cause and just bow-down and accept pain as it is. That is when the friction will be at ease and the pain will subside.

Imagine life's your amusement park—roller coasters, see-saws, and all. Pain? That is the roller coaster, the wild ride that ruffles your hair and races your heart. Success? That is the see-saw, the ride that leaves you grinning ear to ear. Welcome to the "LIFE" amusement park, where your choices fuel the thrills. You are taught to wrestle challenges and seize opportunities. But here is the twist: skipping a challenge or dodging an opportunity—it is a move too. More than grabbing opportunities, bouncing a few is essential. FOMO's that noisy neighbor; sometimes leads us to poor resolutions. It is okay to close the door and savor the quiet. Missed a chance? Lost an opportunity? It is all good, friend. Not every train is meant to be chased; some are better enjoyed from the platform.

In the cosmic barter, you offer to get, you lose to gain, right? But nobody said you have to offer your complete soul in every exchange. Pour some energy into the Universe's cup but save a sip for yourself. Be selective with your investments; not every venture deserves your blood, sweat, and energy because perhaps it is not worth your time. Likewise chose the pains you want to go through, by wise decisions.

Decisions? They are your passports to the pain carnival. Choose your rides wisely. Pain? It is like a tattoo, a story etched beneath your skin. If the tattoo is lovely, it will last otherwise you will opt for laser removal. You need to be wise and cautious as pain changes us on a soul level. Healing? It is your laser-treatment job. Sometimes it sticks, sometimes it is undone. And trust me, you do not want a closet full of unresolved pain trophies. Keep healing.

So, fellow explorer of life, let us be cunning and crafty. Pain's a puzzle, and you are the solver. Embrace it, surrender to it, and dance through it. Remember, not every challenge needs your superhero cape. Pick your battles, and when it is time, bow gracefully and exit the stage. **Life's a performance, my friend—do not just watch it, star in it.**

Actionable Insights: Next time you encounter pain, instead of battling it, try acknowledging it. Name the sensation—"Hey, pain, I see you." This simple act of recognition can create a shift in your perception. It is like waving to a friend rather than ducking away. Remember, pain is not an enemy; it is a messenger. Begin a pain journal. When you face discomfort, jot down your feelings, thoughts, and the situation triggering it. Then, reflect on how you reacted. Over time, you will notice patterns, uncover insights, and develop a new relationship with pain. This journal is not just a record; it is your compass to navigate the labyrinth of growth. Embrace it like a puzzle piece in your life and observe how the picture unfolds.

Hmmm…If you skip opportunities perhaps, you miss discovering the relevant talent in you. Now that is a talk for some-other day. *Think! Because it is all interconnected.*

A Feast Of Words:

You have power to use & choose the pain which comes,

But not when the pain which visits.

Not only the good but also the bad days depend on it.

If vigilant, life is a blessing,

If not, life is a mess again.

Learn to adsorb pain, feel it fully,

Because it is not that the time heals us,

It is that the time we give for pain to heal us.

From "Good Vibes" To "All Vibes Welcome": The Positivity Paradox

Stay positive and let's hope for the best.

"Don't think negative, be positive."

Positive becomes extremely positive,

Be caused by the – "Shadow of positivity."

<u>**Quote says:**</u>

People tend to find positivity in everything and try to be optimistic in life. You do not realize when the same positivity becomes excess and causes negative effects in life without your realization. This is a slow upward curve, which grows without any limit. Slowly, the confidence becomes overconfidence & positivity becomes surplus of positivity.

Imagine this: Your friend Priya walks up to you, her eyes clouded with pain, and says, "Dude, why is life always tough for me? It's tough to be happy." You respond, " "Stay positive Priya, don't think like this." Positivity, like a sprinkle of sunshine on a rainy day, can work wonders. But tread carefully – there is a realm beyond the bright side, a place I call the "Shadow of Positivity" which is the darker side of positivity, which is excess of positivity. Think of it as devouring too much chocolate – excess leading to a loss of charm, echoing Oscar Wilde's wisdom, **"Moderation is a thing. Nothing succeeds if excess."** Have you ever thought why are you asked to stay positive when negativity is the elephant in the room? Isn't it digging good out of the bad?

Let us reflect – why is it that when negativity comes knocking, you are urged to bury it beneath layers of positivity? Isn't this a bit like turning lemons into lemonade? Joy often gets the spotlight, while sorrow remains the shy cousin in the corner. As Brene Brown suggests, "Owning our story can be hard but not nearly as difficult as spending our lives running from it."

Why should the negative aspects of yourself be locked away? Doesn't this stab in the back? The world is so vast. It has both good - bad people, and those have their own good - bad days. Rejecting negativity and only permitting optimism would be like rejecting 50% of the population. What about the negative half of the people? As a consequence of shadow of positivity, you tend to invalidate half of the world. Embracing only sunshine while shunning the rain is like inviting only half of life's party. This, dear friends, is not a fair game.

Let us go deeper. Why cannot suffering just exist without being hidden? **Why must you "stay positive" even when your hearts ache?** You are told to fake it until you make it. It is akin to wearing a beautifully painted mask to conceal a dance of emotions.

If in a situation, your leg bone decides to get hurt, nobody expects you to "Stay Positive." You are rushed to a doctor who knows bones from funny bones. Physical pain gets its due – tears and yelps included. But emotional pain is often brushed aside, hidden behind curtains of positivity. This is where words like suicide and depression find their stage. When pain is suppressed, it simmers and later explodes as depression or heart-wrenching suicides. Teens from as young as fourteen withstand the worst of this harsh reality.

"Good Vibes" is a popular term, but it means "No negativity allowed!" Let us consider a new term – **"All Vibes Welcome."** Imagine a place where negativity is not a pariah, but a guest with its own story.

I admit, I have been down the positivity maze. My Instagram bio once had, **"Good vibes alert!"** But my pillow knew the truth – it soaked up silent cries. Social media, too, plays its part, showcasing only the bright, sunny, and perfect moments.

Actionable Insights:

1. **Embrace Every Hue:** Allow yourself to feel the spectrum of emotions. Acknowledge your shadows as you celebrate your sunshine.
2. **Genuine Listening:** When someone opens up, truly listen. Replace "Stay Positive" with "I'm here for you."
3. **Authentic Sharing:** Break the cycle of picture-perfect appearances. Share your lows alongside your highs, connecting through authenticity.

Remember, life is not a linear journey – it is a symphony of highs and lows, and the magic lies in embracing and finding balance the harmony of both.

Hmmm…How much of positivity is, okay? Where is the line drawn between positivity and its excess? Introspect and create your own limits. *Think! Because it is all interconnected.*

EMBRACING LIFE'S DANCE OF ENDINGS AND BEGINNINGS

We will not meet certain people ever again,

There are ends every day,

There are new starts every day,

Every Moment is a life in a death, in fact.

Quote says:

People change, people's versions get upgraded, no one is the same person as yesterday. Everyone has their own stories and own phases. By the end of the phases, people are new, fresh, different & unique.

Pop Your Bubbles

In the symphony of life, each transition signals the passing of a former self, reminiscent of shedding an old skin. **These moments of change are your mini deaths, steppingstones towards evolution.** Tears, the crystalline manifestations of your emotions, mark a departure as you navigate life's emotional landscape. Even happiness, radiant and effervescent, carries within it a whisper of an ending, much like the fleeting beauty of a sunrise. In this intricate play of existence, your intelligent minds crave the presence of opposites. Just as love finds its dwelling place, so does its shadow, "hate." Happiness and sorrow engage as two sides of the same coin. As Viktor Frankl wisely observed, "Between stimulus and response, there is a space. In that space lies your power to choose your response, and in your response lies your growth and freedom."

You die every time you change,

You die every time you shed a tear,

You die every time you are happy,

You die every time you wake-up to a new day.

Pleasure and pain, contentment, and melancholy—these dualities enrich the tapestry of your emotions. Heraclitus' timeless wisdom reminds us that **you cannot step into the same river twice, for change is the essence of existence.** Within this spectrum, life and its counterpart, death, coexist like two companions linked by an invisible thread.

An intriguing paradox unfolds: **"You live every day. You die every day."** The being you were yesterday, does not exist anymore, we are alive, and we are dead, already. You stand on the threshold of life and death simultaneously, a paradoxical reality. Perhaps each day is a survival of emotional comas, a continuous renewal. You will not meet a friend whom you hurt once, ever again. He has gone along with that pain. You will not be able to feel the same happiness, the same way again. Only time has it with him. You will not meet those strangers who crossed your heart, again. That momentary feel is a memory, already. You will not be able to be a kid again, its wired in you for real. You will not meet this version of yourself again, you are legit dead, already. They all merge into the river of time, becoming footprints etched on its sands. If it happens again, the vibe can be better or less good. But to your boon, your brains' memory is a gift. As you can only live in memories, again. You can only bring that feeling again, in your memory. You need to cherish them.

Recapturing the innocence of childhood is an elusive feat; that era of wide-eyed wonder remains forever beyond your grasp. With each passing moment, you bid farewell to the version of yourself that existed. As I type these words, this very instant becomes history. Yet, within your grasp lies the ability to resurrect memories, to relive moments anew.

All things conclude in life, including life itself. This enigma infuses life with excitement and purpose. While the ends of other stories are known, life's conclusion remains an enigmatic surprise. Likewise, is life but with an unknown end. When you watch a movie which obviously will end, do you stop watching it or living it? You embrace it more fervently due to its impending end. So be it with life and its experiences but with an end, which can come anytime. Yet life's experiences remain indefinite in their definiteness. Hug and live every bit of it because it will end and so will you.

Life's value is doubled infinite times, once you realize that "It won't ever happen again, in real time." Only what you cannot see, hear, feel, or again has value to you; the rest is taken for granted. When an awaited new movie is released, you are excited, but you know that you still can re-watch it anytime later, that is why you are okay with missing it. In life, to immortalize memories amid shifting sands, must you master the art of **"Living in the present"**? As Eckhart Tolle advises, **"Realize deeply that the present moment is all you ever have."** Embrace the ebb and flow of endings and beginnings. Each chapter of life's story is a step in the dance of change. Cherish the finite moments, for they make life's melody unforgettable.

Actionable Insights: Dedicate a few minutes each day to practicing mindfulness. Find a quiet space, sit comfortably, and focus on your

Pop Your Bubbles

breath. Pay attention to each inhale and exhale. When your mind inevitably drifts to thoughts of the past or future, gently bring it back to the present moment—the sensation of your breath, the sounds around you, and the feeling of being alive right now.

Hmmm…To cherish these memories long after things change, should you not learn to **"Live in the present"**? *Think! Because it is all interconnected.*

THE PERCEPTION PUZZLE: UNMASKING THE INTRICATE WEB OF IMPRESSIONS AND JUDGMENTS

"She has good amount of knowledge & is smarter."

"I don't like the energy we share."

Is your perception about someone.

"She shouldn't have cheated on him."

"She is not doing it right. Her approach is wrong."

"Look at the way she walks."

Is how you are passing judgmental comments & being less kind.

<u>Quote says:</u>

Being judgmental is getting you nowhere & helping you in no way. It is just making you less of a human.

Pop Your Bubbles

Have you ever been caught in a whirlwind of judgment, even as the teachings of non-judgment echo in your mind? Life's enigmatic twists sometimes throw us into a paradox, right? Yet not every assessment is a definitive judgment; some are mere initial brushstrokes on the canvas of understanding. Just like getting to know their names, you build some first impressions about the person. First impressions are helpful to know who a person is or what is expected out of him. First impression is the first step & judgment is the second step in knowing someone.

Picture stepping onto a dance floor where the first move is impression, the spark of connection. It is the moment you sense someone's energy, their style, their voice – a fleeting snapshot of who they might be. "Their enthusiasm is infectious!" or "Her fashion sense is an art." These swift notes set the stage for unraveling a person's story which are the first impressions.

As time unfurls chapters beyond the cover, the judgments you pen are like twists in a compelling tale. Think of it as critiquing a novel – praising a chapter's brilliance or noting a misplaced plot turn. It is your perspective, a commentary, not the final verdict. Imagine your favorite movie – its intricate plot, stunning visuals, and moving performances. Now, what if a friend dismisses that movie? If you condemn him, "Your taste in movies needs to evolve." You have ventured into judgment territory. Instead, celebrate their unique cinematic journey – a path to embracing empathy.

But why do judgments slip from your lips as if carved in stone? It is as if you are peeling layers of an onion, revealing the core within. Often, judgments arise from your internal turbulence – a stormy sea of self-doubt and preconceptions. When your inner narrative is unresolved, you become judgmental critics for others. Judgment is when you force or label any deed as wrong or right just because it is wrong or right in your experience. **Validating or invalidating anyone based in your experience is judgment.**" Pranay was wrong, he should not have done this to Riya." Is a judgmental comment. Just because what he did is wrong in your experience, you must not label that Pranay is wrong, perhaps even Riya might think he is right, you do not know.

Why do you judge or force your judgement on others?

You tend to judge because you are not in peace with yourself, unkind to yourself, have lot of stereotypes intact in you, have not accepted and judge yourself too. You can accept others only if you know how to accept yourself. When your judge others, you feel much valued and capable of yourself. If you pass a prejudice on someone in a crowd, won't you feel included or valued? People just are running behind filling their empty inner selves. Imagine glimpsing a "6" while another sees a "9" in the same scene. It is about perspective. You are a wanderer marveling at different facets of a multifaceted gem. Until you understand this, judgments continue to fill life's margins. Visualize your inner self as a curious child, yearning to be heard. You have jailed those parts of yourself, generating internal chaos. How you treat others reflects how you treat yourself – slices of the same judgment-laden cake.

Consider this: You evaluate others based on their actions, but yourself based on your intentions. It is like measuring with two different yardsticks. Every action carries a hidden backstory – a fusion of experiences and thoughts. When you judge, you shift from curious explorers to courtroom judges – handing out verdicts without grasping the entire case. Each journey is a unique tapestry woven from experiences, lessons, strengths, and vulnerabilities. It is a treasure hunt, with everyone seeking to fill their personal void.

"Our job is not to judge, but to be kind, even when it's tough." — Josh Radnor

Remember, you all emerge from stardust, destined to return to it. Amid this cosmic journey, you are characters in a symphony of experiences. Your stories intertwine, threads woven by the Universe. Sometimes you harmonize, other times you contrast vividly. It is all part of the same masterpiece.

As I share these musings, remember that they may resonate differently with you – a reflection of your unique melody. Let us be as malleable as clay, reshaping our perceptions as life evolves. For the question of gut feelings and instincts – that is a mystery you will explore in chapters to come.

Actionable Insights: The next time you are about to judge, pause and wonder about the hidden story behind the action. Challenge yourself to unravel layers beneath the surface. Just as your story weaves from experiences, so does theirs. Practicing empathy leads you to a more open-hearted perspective.

What about the instincts and the gut feeling? That is a question for the next round then. *Think! Because it is all interconnected.*

UNVEILING THE AUTHENTIC SOUL: A JOURNEY OF CREATIVE LIBERATION

Why fear, being judged?

Two people can rarely be similar.

But will never be the same.

Everyone is unique,

Everything is subjective,

Why spit prejudices?

<u>Quote Says:</u>

When everyone has their own stories and phases, their own good and bad days, everyone will have nothing as "same" but just as "similar." You might be able to relate to somebody's story, but you can never feel and experience it in their shoes or feel the same. Everyone behaves as they do because of the wiring that happened to them on a personal level. If they commit deeds because they feel that way, their past had control over it. Their past encounters had coerced them to do them, and it cannot be edited anyway.

Pop Your Bubbles

Example: People are out of control when they are in anger, which is their past ruling over them. It just cannot be edited until the past is modified. Why to judge them while they are deserted and powerless already? The next time when you judge someone, just say "He must be having some story behind it" to yourself. An anger which is in control of the person and doesn't overpower, is not influenced by the past wiring. Such a person has got control over his anger.

In a world where blogging and Instagram held realms of creative possibility, I also explored my creativity via writing @authorsaloni blogs about life. My heart thrummed with an unyielding passion for words – an unquenchable desire to weave stories and craft poems that resonated with the essence of human experience. However, within the vibrant tapestry of her creative pursuits, an insidious shadow loomed me– the ever-persistent fear of judgment. As I poised myself to unveil my fertile creativity, a cascade of uncertainties surged within me, will my loyal followers applaud or forsake me for my authenticity.

Amid the embryonic days of my journey, my fingers wavered in doubt while I wrote, thinking about reader's judgements. A staggering 90% of my compositions underwent transformations to conform as per my audience desired. I was in a loop of validation-seeking. My natural voice, a resonant echo of my inner self, got gradually overwritten with edits to blend seamlessly with perceived expectations.

Each post bore witness to a subtle tug-of-war – a struggle between the pursuit of authenticity and the gravitational pull of conformity. As if a puppeteer manipulating my strings, I contorted my words to mirror expected reactions, inadvertently erasing the radiant hues of my distinctive essence. Yet, these modified verses stood as silent witnesses to my evolution, recounting tales of transformation, growth, and profound self-discovery. After some days of shit-posting, I was realizing all this was going nowhere, I felt pressured, struggled to express myself instead of feeling happy, writing. I stopped posting for a while.

Then, akin to a phoenix arising from the ashes of self-doubt, a profound shift unfolded within me. I embarked on a journey of rediscovery, an expedition to redefine my relationship with my creativity and to transcend the waves of judgment. In my quest for inner fortitude, I stumbled upon an anecdote which recounted the transformative training of army cadets in which they were asked to get stripped in front of all other army aspirants, where vulnerability was not merely tolerated, but embraced as a catalyst for growth. This said, on a basic level everyone is, has and does the same. Each of us have a heart, a pair of eyes, ears, hands, legs, and kidneys; this struck me hard. Realizing this, I said to myself, **"Saloni, why fear people who are no different."** Everybody shits and pees in life, like you do. Just that people talk and show or hide parts of themselves. Nobody is open to express everything. It is just the acquired materials over the lifetime that people look vile, judgmental, insane, and different. Everyone has come from a mother's womb, had cried, laughed, committed mistakes, had regrets, heartbreaks, pain etc. Next, I changed forever. This parable resonated within my core, illuminating the darkest corners of my fear. Emboldened by this newfound epiphany, I cast aside the chains of judgment, embracing my raw, unfiltered essence with unwavering determination.

With newfound resolve, I confronted my words once more. This time, words flowed as a river unbridled, cascading forth with unrestrained force. With a steady breath, I pressed "Enter," propelling my thoughts into the boundless digital expanse. No second-guessing, no edits to dilute the vibrant hues of authenticity. It was my voice – untamed, untethered, and unapologetic. In that ephemeral moment, I savored the intoxicating freedom of liberation, akin to a bird soaring upon the winds of limitless possibility.

The response was enchanting. My engagement surged and followers multiplied, yet the most profound reward was the tranquility that enfolded my heart. With each post, I reveled my uniqueness, finding solace in my unwavering, authentic expression. Empowered by newfound confidence, I ascended to even greater heights till this authored book, with self-assuredness. As I glanced back, my heart swelled with a mixture of satisfaction and pride. The fear of judgment, which had once cast a shadow over my path, had been vanquished, replaced by an indomitable spirit of self-discovery.

Pop Your Bubbles

Actionable Insights: Recognize that being open and authentic in your creative work can lead to more meaningful and satisfying expressions. Focus on the tone of your fingers rather than seeking external approval. Understand that everyone has fears, doubts, and imperfections, making judgment less intimidating. Allow your unique voice and perspective to shine through in your creative endeavors.

Hmmm... What if while I overcome the fear of judgment, I lose the capability to sense wrong deeds? Well, that is a talk for another day. *Think! Because it is all interconnected.*

THREADS OF UNDERSTANDING: UNRAVELING STEREOTYPES IN THE MIDST OF DIVERSITY

People design their own masks and barely wear it.

They later, flex about the masks' design and force it unto you.

Also design new masks, again; it is a loop, for real.

Masks are the stereotypes.

Kill the Stereotypes.

<u>*Quote says:*</u>

Masks are the rules and policies, the validations, or patterns in life. There are multiple rules and regulations to live in a country but more than those decree, there are steps and stretches to dress-up, daily living, fashion, female looks and male looks, dining, grooming, temples etc. These need to be killed because they make our lives harder. Etiquettes are good but not the stereotypes.

Pop Your Bubbles

Embarking on my journey into the professional world with a role at KPMG in Bengaluru, I found myself stepping out of the corona-era's haze in 2021. Hybrid work was becoming the new norm, and as I settled into a women's PG near the office, little did I know that a series of events would reshape my perceptions forever.

One day, amidst the routine, an unexpected turn of events unfolded. The PG manager asked me to move to a different room, a change that led me to stumble upon an unexpected sight. In a ladies' PG, I encountered a young man asleep beneath a blanket in that room. Startled, I hurriedly reported this breach to the PG manager. She joined me in the room only to find it empty, leaving us both, baffled. In that room, an array of feminine garments hung on the walls, baffling me further. My hasty assumptions about the individual's gender came crashing down. I questioned my initial judgment. What if this was a "she" and not a "he"? I chose to suspend judgment until I had more information and waited in the room for the young man to be back.

Soon, the individual returned, and with a flutter of uncertainty, I ventured a conversation. "When did you join this PG?" I inquired. He said, "Yeah, this morning and already, looks like someone mis-took me to be a guy because of my hairdo and has complained, I'm a proud woman yaar but these stereotypical people, gosh! Uh!" The response, in a gentle, feminine tone, struck a chord. I was banging my head in my mind and just said, "oh!" We started to share a good bond and stamped ground a lot, she also talked about her stories and that how it is a struggle for her to survive in this rude-stereotypical world. She recounted on how her pixie hairstyle peeping from the blanket at the first sight had led to mistaken assumptions about her gender. This encounter, prompted profound introspection on the pervasiveness of stereotypes, ingrained from birth, shaping our understanding of **'right'** and **'wrong.'** I was introspecting about how deep the stereotypes are rooted in us. From birth, we have been taught them. We are showed and exposed to those repeatedly that your photographic memory only validates that as right and rest to be wrong or to be changed. Only the first moment we were born; we were not with any stereotypical filter, the next moment, everyone we meet or see, has knowingly or unknowingly given many stereotypes. **It is** unlimited; it indulges in our emotional validations and confidence.

Guess, how worlds' fashion is set? No offence to the fashion freaks, but this is just an analogous example. Shoutout to the world of fashion for their humongous efforts. The fashion industry designs a quantity of weird outfits, in spite of knowing that a person cannot wear it. How did the trend of pastel colors begin? Pastel colors look so dull & pale at first. Think of light brown, it would look like shit. But the fashion industry needs to make us wear it and for that to happen they need to market and make sure people like it, as well. Hence, they give all those awkward outfits to the influencers, celebrities and other people who will cross our eyes, every now and then. Eventually when you are exposed to these regularly by the people who are known as the fashion gods, the outfit ideas are sold to us. Just like the reels on Instagram which are repeatedly fed so many times that you start adhering to it whether you like it or not.

Initially you criticize, then you slowly accept the trend looking at other common people wearing them and later start liking it. Multiple times, you must have seen the people who are not in the influence of social apps or the fashion trends, like our parents for instance, will remark "What kind of outfit or color is this?" when we present ourselves with those weird stuffs on us. If we keenly observe, this is how the stereotypes are sent to us and we fall for it; without even realizing. What sort a fashion is torn jean? Or is a torn top? Will we accept the fashion sense of a girl who is old fashioned or call her beautiful, in this changed trend? Obviously, not. Perhaps, she likes to wear it and she does, proudly or she is from a dull background or cannot afford it and hence does not wear the stereotypes you wear. You might label her "*ugly*" but is it right to deny her existence, just because she is off trend? Look at the emotional invalidation and timidity you set for her? Think, how many would have been through this because you wore certain other stereotypes. **This is the effect of the stereotypes just around the fashion industry, there are million other domains in the world.**

The phenomenon extends to social media. The sway of platforms like Instagram is undeniable – a mundane song becomes a sensation through the magic of reels. Influencers jump on trends, ensuring repeated exposure. This is how repetitive re-watch makes us mirror and like it. In our brains, we have the mirror neurons which mirrors what we see & hear. The mirror neurons are there in us from birth, which is why when you look at a baby and smile, it smiles as well. This **'Mirroring'** stems from our mirror neurons, reflecting what we see and hear, often leading us to embrace what initially seemed odd.

The deeper truth is this: **Anything that defies logic is likely a stereotype.** Of course, there is science beyond logic which is in the process of discovery but that's not the kind of logic I'm referring to. Our behavior varies based on where we are – alone, with family, friends, or a crowd – all shaped by the stereotypes we have absorbed. I'm speaking of the stereotypes framed in our minds which are on no humanitarian grounds and are also less beneficial to the surrounding lives. The maximum number of stereotypes or labels are sent across, while we are in a group. Each one in the group will pose one or multiple pattern they know and without even a question you will adhere to it, just because you know that person and it is a group which means safety, truth & herd mentality. In one group sitting, you are sold to a list of certain accepted ideas which will accept you and validate you. However, these biases are not indelible. Shedding them demands conscious effort.

There are forms of yourself you see, the ones when you are alone, with family, with friends & in the crowd and I bet no version is the same. This is because of the of stereotypes which are increasing even now. Imagine, how many other stereotypes are sticking unto you. Shed the patterns, stereotypes, labels as and when you realize. Learn to be kind and baby hearted, accept the differences, this life is an opportunity, you have got & so has everyone else. As you navigate life, remember that not all stereotypes are inherently negative. Some streamline daily functioning, but others hinder growth. Embrace the power to discern between the two. What truly matters is change from within. **Challenge the stereotypes that limit your potential and embrace those that broaden your perspective.** This process sparks personal growth and cultivates empathy. In the end, our journey is about embracing diversity, dismantling preconceptions, and building an inclusive world. A world where you actively shape perceptions, for yourselves and those you encounter.

Actionable Insights:

Challenge Your Stereotypes: Embrace the power to discern between stereotypes that limit potential and those that broaden perspectives. Shed the patterns, labels, and biases as you recognize them. Be kind, open-hearted, and accept differences.

Understand the Power of Influence: Recognize that many stereotypes are shaped by external influences, like the fashion industry or social media trends. When exposed to unconventional ideas repeatedly, your brain adapts.

Mirror Wisely: Remember that your behavior often mirrors those around you. In groups, stereotypes and patterns can be reinforced. Challenge these ideas and encourage open-mindedness.

Hmmm… Are all stereotypes bad? If all are bad, then a man should be treated like a woman is. But that's not the case. *Think! Because it is all interconnected.*

A Feast Of Words:

There are forms of "us" we see,

We are different with dissimilar things,

We are different with diverse humans,

Not that it is deceptive to be so.

We choose our homies, we choose our form of "us," always.

It is enthralling, unique energies spring up extra-ordinary parts of us.

And distinctive humans see unique forms of us,

Just like as if a human power could simulate the rains,

Just like a superpower which keeps on increasing.

10.

THE LONELINESS-BOREDOM TANGO: CRAFTING A SYMPHONY OF SELF-DISCOVERY

Feeling bored?

Binge watch, Text people, Talk to a friend.

Feeling bored?

Eat food, Go Hangout, Sleep.

Feeling bored?

Listen to Music, Go on a ride.

The cycle repeats.

Feeling bored or are you feeling lonely?

<u>**Quote says:**</u>

Boredom is a constant, it will always be there. Anything can be replaced instead of boredom, it will still be back the next day, like the sunrises every day, boredom will never fail to rise again and so is loneliness.

Picture a world where loneliness is a companion you meet along the way – not a foe to avoid, but an opportunity to explore. And then there's boredom, that mischievous friend who nudges you into seeking new adventures. **Loneliness is forever.** Boredom is forever and is the other name of loneliness, in some cases. If there is peace made with loneliness, boredom is just wanting something to do. Boredom is when we feel restless being idle. Being idle and bored means there is no fun element in being with self. We are not enjoying our own company, isn't it?

Imagine, for a moment, that boredom is a puzzle piece, and loneliness is the frame that holds it all together. When you make peace with your solitude, boredom transforms from an adversary into a catalyst. It is like having a friend who is always ready to venture into the unknown with you. **But why are you so uncomfortable in stillness?**

You are spontaneous & impulsive that you just avoid spending time with your inner child. You do not like your own company, but you like to be with friends, how is that possible? If you cannot be with yourself, how will the other person manage to be with you? While you are just waiting for someone to arrive, you keep nagging your phones, as if you've got big commitments. **I mean look at the how much you want to be away from yourself.** Now-a-days, you have numerous options to get occupied with, to worsen this, you have a fidget spinner, as well. You can easily avoid boredom or loneliness with all of this.

You need a reason to live,

You need someone to connect with,

You need passion or hobby,

You are foodie, binge watch, sleep, listen to Music, go on a ride etc.

Do you see, what I see?

That we want to keep ourselves busy.

We just do not want to feel empty or idle.

Pop Your Bubbles

But think! When avoiding boredom, brings it up again, isn't it a better or wise choice to make peace with it/accept it? Learn to accept boredom, by spending time in boredom; spend time with self.

Spending time with self is like knowing yourself, you sit across from your own thoughts, like old friends catching up after years apart. This is the art of solitude – **a date with your soul**. It is about being comfortable in your own skin, acknowledging yourself and relishing the conversations you have with your thoughts. **Remember being a child, lost in the wonder of your own imagination?** It is time to reconnect with that part of you. Embrace the spontaneity, the curiosity, and the joy that your inner child offers. Nurture it by spending quality time alone, engaging in activities that light up your soul.

Ever noticed that the elders around us might be better at this. They can spend time idle, doing nothing and fidgeting nothing at all. That is what is spending time with self like. It is a lesson in reconnecting with oneself, a reminder that the art of solitude is a gift we often overlook. Spending time chatting with our mind or thoughts and cutting out from the world to just peep in, to let the inner child express what it needs or wants. More than how we were treated in our past, how we treat ourselves, shapes us. **Thoughts keep crossing our mind, every second.** We have an extremely chattering mind because we do not listen to ourselves. We do not attend the inner child in us which craves so much attention from us and deserves it as well. When we do not listen to self and be there for ourselves, we feel restless, alone, needing for someone to divert us. Our mind or the inner child never fails to stop trying to talk with us, we still do not take efforts to listen or respond that clingy child. Are you aware of your strengths, weakness, voids, likes, dislikes, patterns, thoughts, dreams, wants, needs, versions, pains, past, self? Introspect with honesty. We do not know even the basics of ourselves, yet. To know anyone, we spend time with them, right? Same should be valid here, to know you, be with you. It is high time we realize this because we do not know where or why are we going. We are in the herd mentality. Even if we think we are unique and not in the herd, we are in that chunk, of that type of a herd. This world with all its multiple octopus like hands has everything ready to make us really unsteady and pull us into its influence. We need to realize this and work on ourselves. **Go on a date with self, you will be glad.**

There is no limit to knowing oneself, it is always extending, but being known of what can be expected out of you from this version & where you are with yourself is the key. Making peace with loneliness is not easy, it is accepting that we will be alone, we only have ourselves for us, we cannot extract connection out of anyone. Nobody is liable to make us happy. **Only you can fill your void.** It is spending time with self, being a friend to the self and having all the conversations, be it hard, sad, vulnerable, happy, tough, awkward, unreal, fun etc. which will help us be contended with self. That is when the connection with self will be restored, and the loneliness will begin to wither away. If we try to extract joy or happiness from others, it is like eating our favorite chocolate because we crave for it. At first, its bliss, but the craving returns and this time the craving will be for more. Seeking happiness from external sources is a similar cycle. It is like trying to quench your thirst with a sieve. Until we are eating the chocolate, we feel good and happy, by the end we may not be satisfied as well; but once the chocolate is over, for some time we will be good, later we will crave for a new one, from the same person or a new person and this time the craving will be more. If this craving and gratification is happening from an external resource, repeatedly; imagine the level of craving which is increased exponentially. **We are stuck in the loop of cravings.**

When we are physically hurt, only thing we crave for is medical aid, to heal the hurt. We crave to feel free from the physical pain via medical aid. While we crave for this aid, we cannot of think of anything else, any other problem or other goals in life. We just are a slave to this craving, so is emotional craving and dissatisfaction which is in loop enslaving us. Emotional pain can be like an itch we cannot ignore. But instead of scratching that itch externally, know that satisfying our craving should not be the goal, we need to grow beyond and uncouple from those endless cravings. **We need to program our mind and heal from the triggering past.** This will put an end to the overpowering cravings. Only if we know, understand and be there for self we will regain our power and buckle down our cravings.

Think of yourself as a garden. Just as a garden needs care and attention, so do you. Spend time in solitude, nourishing the soil of your thoughts. Weed out negativity, water the seeds of positivity, and watch your inner garden flourish. Imagine you are crafting your own story – one where you are the protagonist. As you spend time in solitude, you are penning the chapters of your life. It is a journey of empowerment, a way to reclaim the narrative from the distractions that seek to hijack it. Picture solitude as your sanctuary – a refuge from the chaos outside. Here, you are free to explore the corridors of your mind, to listen to the whispers of your heart. It is a space to dance with your thoughts, to listen to your dreams, and to be your own best friend.

Actionable Insights: Embrace solitude as a friend, not a foe. Unravel the mysteries of boredom and let it lead you to new adventures within yourself. It is a journey worth taking.

Hmmm… Don't you think all the businesses in the world are successful because of the cravings we have and if we do not long for anything, businesses will not function as much. *Think! Because it is all interconnected.*

11.

FROM IDOLS TO REALITIES: NAVIGATING THE SPECTRUM OF INFLUENCE

Admire people, Cherish people,

Celebrate people, Congratulate people,

Wish people, Get inspired.

But do not look up-to people,

Do not look down on people,

Just look at people as they are.

Quote says:

There are bountiful amount people who are at a greater position in life, today; and you admire them, feel inspired by them, wish to learn them and be like them. You start to want to take after them as a whole and look at them in a hierarchical pace, but you need to look at them (people) in a horizontal manner.

Pop Your Bubbles

Amid life's endless narrative you start look up to the people & admire for their skills but in this process, you start to build fantasies around those people & place them at a post where you would place the highest. Our gaze often ascends toward certain individuals, captivated by their extraordinary talents. Then you begin to look up-to them in every aspect and want to be fully like them, including their weaknesses subconsciously. Now, this journey of admiration takes a curious turn. It is like a painting, where you start adding vibrant brushstrokes to these people, elevating them to the highest peaks within our imagination. Every facet of their existence becomes a North Star guiding us toward emulation, sometimes even inheriting their vulnerabilities without realizing. Extreme admiration makes us all do the trite stuffs they do. Imagine being drawn to someone's humility, but the same person might gamble in a casino at nights, not that it is a crime, but that you do not know about the full picture. Suddenly, that gambling habit becomes oddly fascinating, a trait you are tempted to adopt. Because of the heavy influencing power of the top celebrities; they represent advertisements, to help in quick marketing. A person in power can sell anything and a person in admiration and inspiration, can be sold to them. You need to just pick and adhere from people & never adopt them in yourself.

"Admiration adds color to our canvas, but a touch of realism keeps us grounded." - Samuel West

Same goes with the people we dislike; we look down on them & treat them low. Do you know that, we could have been in that position anytime and since we are not (in our mind); we have not got the authority to illtreat them. We are in peoples' good and bad stories. It is a paradigm shift - just because we haven't walked in their shoes doesn't justify belittling them. We are all characters woven into each other's stories, sometimes the protagonists, sometimes the antagonists.

"Before you judge, walk a mile in someone else's shoes." - Mary Williams

Consider this: Would you appreciate receiving the same treatment you sometimes dole out to those you regard as 'lesser'? They are human, like you, with their own tales and trials. Within their stories may lie priceless wisdom. Even the humblest house cleaner might hold insights beyond your imagination's reach.

Shift your perspective, viewing every individual on a level playing field. **Each person, navigating life's maze, confronting challenges and victories uniquely.** The qualities that draw us to our idols often mirror the attributes you wish to embody or have cherished in the past. Take people in a horizontal manner; everyone out here is a human and is struggling to maneuver through life. Everyone out here is unique and everyone knows more or less than we know. Be kind, entrust respect and humanity.

If you imbibe and understand that you are all in a horizontal pace, when you grow to greater a position later in life, you will not tend to build the ego of being great or feel like the king and not look down on the rest. You will feel that horizontal pace and will continue to look at people the same way with greatness. This is an important learning to adhere in life, now or later.

"Life is a symphony of stories; every soul contributes a unique note." - Ava Thompson

Every individual possesses a treasure trove of insights, varying in depth yet equally valuable. Kindness, respect, and shared humanity form the threads knitting our shared existence. By adopting this panoramic outlook, as we ascend to new heights, our ego need not inflate. This journey forms an unending cycle, and as you progress, the richness of each individual's narrative becomes vivid.

Actionable Insights: When you catch yourself admiring or judging, pause. Embrace the traits that resonate, while honoring the fact that each person, including you, contributes a unique melody to the orchestra of existence. Let kindness guide you. This wisdom is not bound by time; it is a beacon that illuminates the present and the future. *Think! Because it's all interconnected.*

12.

SCULPTING YOUR SOUL: CRAFTING RESPONSES BEYOND PERSONALITY LABELS

Want to consult a doctor? Be patient.

Waiting for results? Be patient.

Pursuing a goal or start-up? Be patient.

Anything happens? Be patient?

No, do not generalize it.

Quote says:

In life, we need to apply our learnings and habits, appropriately. You should not generalize your learnings across all the life decisions, opportunities, or circumstances. Sometimes life might demand the furious you, other times it might demand the calmer version of you, if you show furiousness or calmness to every circumstance, things will fall out of place, and you will not even know how because in your mind you will think you are right. We tend to generalize everything.

We are often handed a conclusion on a silver platter and told, "If this arises, this is your cue." This neat formula becomes our blueprint for dealing with any situation – we call it our "nature" or "personality." But just like that, in the past, someone crowned us "the patient one" and left the label stuck like a stubborn sticker.

Picture this: You are at a social gathering, and suddenly, you are christened "the patient guru." This label shadows you like a loyal puppy, following you through conversations and gatherings. Gradually, it molds into a part of your identity – you are now the reigning monarch of patience. But think about this - the tale of the tortoise and the hare is not just about speed; it is about the right response at the right time.

Let us conjure a scenario: An impending project deadline is on your neck. Thanks to the "patient guru" tag, you stay patient despite the deadline. Yet, as the finish line nears, logic whispers working on it as quick as possible is the expected response. Alas, your to-do list queues up, and your task threatens to remain incomplete, leading to potential disqualification – like to stumble before the finish line.

Speaking of wild scenarios, imagine a lion in the room. Logic screams that patience would be folly, considering lions do not usually RSVP for tea. Now shift gears: Guests are enroute, but the meal is not ready. Patience becomes your ally as you wait for the food, playing host and making their wait enjoyable with tasty food and not half cooked food. Franklin P. Jones once quipped, **"Patience has its limits. Take it too far, and its cowardice."** Life's a mosaic where each tile demands a unique response. Sometimes, only patience can wield its magic, while impatience is a tantrum in vain.

Let's consider kindness in the place of patience. Kindness, an essential part of us, blooms in various hues. But here is a plot twist: showering kindness on a toxic relationship can be a recipe for self-destruction. Just as kindness is commendable, standing up for us is vital. **Without self-respect, we become doormats, collecting dust as the world walks over us.** Protecting our dignity safeguards us from the trauma of poor choices. Here is the secret: **respond, do not react.** As Charles R. Swindoll aptly put it, "Life is 10% what happens to us and 90%

how we react to it." Prioritize, act wisely, and let your actions echo your true self.

Golden rule: Stop wearing personalities like costumes. Stop labelling oneself with personalities, you need to get rid of all the masks you wear in the name of our personality. Personalities are like our resume which is written more by others and less by us. **Do not curate a resume of qualities; life's not a one-size-fits-all affair.** If you chose patience in a situation, do not immediately label oneself as "Patient." You need not build a resume of nature of how you are, and these are your qualities. This resume will not be useful in places where the job role is different. Even for jobs we need a subjective degree, skills. All skills are not valid for any role we want. We need to respond wisely & do what we should do.

Actionable Insights: When the label temptation strikes, pause. Reflect on whether your default response aligns with the moment's demand. **Just as a chef picks spices, choose your reaction.** Do not limit yourself – experiment with assorted flavors of response, just as you would try on new outfits. After all, you are not one costume: you're a wardrobe of choices.

What if you reach a state where you associate with no labels at all, you become free of restrictions and titles. That's when you experience freedom. Freedom is not getting rid of responsibilities but being responsibly free of labels and stereotypes. *Think! Because its interconnected.*

THE ESSENCE OF LIVING: NAVIGATING LIFE'S THREE PERSPECTIVES

Life is never a race,

Life is not a game,

It is just a journey with a purpose or

It is just a journey without a purpose.

Quote says:

Life is not a challenge or a competition, it is a journey rather. It is just a travel wherein we go through various places (phases) and learn different stuffs, learn about the phases, and feel mesmerized with how magnificent life is.

Pop Your Bubbles

If life were a royal race with a finish line to pursue? our focus narrows onto certain deadlines and goals. Yet, do these self-imposed finish lines obscure the vibrant landscapes and hidden trails we pass by? Just as a ship confined to a predetermined course misses the uncharted waters teeming with potential discoveries.

In this relentless pursuit, shared humanity often fades from view. Maya Angelou reminds us, "We all should know that diversity makes for a rich tapestry." Jealousy simmers, success becomes a measuring factor against others. Our frantic dash can lead us to shortcuts and Helen Keller's wisdom echoes, **"Character cannot be developed in ease and quiet. Only through experience of trial and suffering can the soul be strengthened."** We will not explore the rest of the opportunities because we are already bound & cannot deviate. You will feel jealous of every other successful person and look for cheat options. You will look at the other humans in your life as competitors and not less or more than that. We will start looking at other humans as vile. **Being humans, where is the humanity, here?** What if, our life ends, striving for the goal & when you look back there will be nothing that we will be able to cherish about. But in our single-minded chase, the thread of our shared humanity frays, and those around us become mere competitors.

If life were a game of chess? Much like we ponder an opponent's next move on the board, do you find yourself consumed by predicting other's actions? You will only be interested in others next move; we will have our copious focus in figuring out that move which the opponent will make. You will tend to make your move based on what the opponent will make. It will turn out to be a game of gamble. Our entire life will never be about us and you will start to fear checkmates at each other's move. You will fear meeting other people. Your moves become reactions, driven by a fear of being outwitted. This existence mirrors a gamble where we wager our identity, aspirations, and potential connections. **Where is "life" in such a life?** It is just like a rat race. It will bring about more challenge between two humans, rather than humanity. If our life expires, in the mid-play, we will be replaced with a next opponent, the next second. Can you see the abundance of lifelessness prevailing here? **Life was never meant to be a game.**

Now, envision life as a profound journey, with or without a destiny, you will be able to enjoy every here and now. Think of it as Paulo Coelho's **"The Alchemist, "Where the journey, not the destination, harbors the magic."** With each step, we gather stories, emotions, and connections, much like travelers amass mementos along the way. Consider Anne Lamott's suggestion, "Almost everything will work if you unplug it for a few minutes, including you." We will be able to feel, react, collect memories, connect to people, be humane & make the most out of the moment. You will look at the other humans as a co-passenger hosting their own voyage. Detaching from the rush allows us to discover the value of each moment. People around us cease to be competitors; they evolve into fellow explorers, each on a unique path. Ralph Waldo Emerson once mused, **"Life is a journey, not a destination."**

The moments you inhabit matter more than the goals you chase. The journey itself, not just the milestones, becomes your teacher. You will not have to fear the end, you will be able to accept death at any time. Even if you die the next moment, you will be thankful for the life you lived, than for the goals you worked for. The focus will be all on you tackling your stuff, and you will learn every day. On this voyage, death is not an adversary; it is a reminder to wholeheartedly embrace life. As the Stoic philosopher Seneca advises, **"Begin at once to live, and count each separate day as a separate life."** You will enjoy yourself because you feel livelier when it comes out of love for the life you live. You learn to love yourself, celebrate growth, and sway to life's rhythm. If you are devoid of goals in life, it is okay to be so because life is a journey to be enjoyed. If you do have a goal in life, it is okay to be so because life is a journey and your life has a destination in the mind (not in real life yet) you will strive towards it while you enjoy the progress towards the goal. Here your journey is a little modified than the other with a goal, and you will live life via living it. It is a journey to be enjoyed towards the goal.

Then the **"Purposes"** in life are like a cherry on top of the cake. We can have it or not; or have it any form as well, it is completely our choice. We can enjoy our journey with our purpose as well. We can have varied goals & strive for it, while reminding ourselves that the life which might become a competition to us as we adapt to the goals is a journey to be lived. The whole point here is to just learn and not to forget to feel lively and live life, while you hustle and struggle. If you do so, you will never fail to admit "life Is beautiful" by the end of the day.

At the end having a purpose is less significant and is subjective but being a responsible human is a baseline responsibility of every living person on Earth. You may or may not contribute to the world in terms of your goals as your purpose but to be human – being kind, helpful, generous, lovable etc. is the prime responsibility because that's your Karma and Dharma.

Actionable Insights: Reflect on the experiences and connections you encountered. Release the urge to compare or strategize. Instead, immerse yourself in the richness of the present.

If you don't commit good deeds (follow your Dharma) you won't have a balance sheet with good karma henceforth, life won't reward a good experience to you as well. As life energy knows exactly what you deserve. *Think! Because its interconnected.*

(Skip, if the previous part (karma/dharma) is a little overboard. It's okay, learning is got to be a little confusing, if I'm not the right teacher for you, someone else will definitely teach you. Move on!)

SOULFUL HARMONY: NAVIGATING THE BOND BETWEEN BODY AND SOUL

You are your soul,

You are the HOME for your soul,

That is where you feel at home.

That is where you will feel at peace.

If your soul sneezes, the body will feel cold.

If your soul feels ache, the body will feel the pain.

Because you are your soul.

You need to learn to live with it.

Quote says:

As multiple souls reside in one home in the physical world, we (our souls) are born within our homes and that is where our peace and happiness lie. Looking for peace, happiness, sadness, joy, pleasure, satisfaction anywhere outside, will make you more ungratified, disrupted, and mentally homeless. That is why we need to feel contended with ourselves, then take external tolls in life. In the heart of our existence resides the soul – an ethereal essence that calls our body its home. This vessel we inhabit is the sacred abode of our innocent soul, a union that is as captivating as it is profound. The soul's embrace of our existence is both a privilege and a responsibility, one that urges us to safeguard this tender connection.

Pop Your Bubbles

There are times when we unknowingly drift away from our soul, perhaps even denying its significance. Yet, beneath the surface, our soul remains steadfast in its devotion. It yearns for us, craves our presence, an eternal companion that shares in our joys, guards our secrets, and steadfastly stands by us. When solitude engulfs us, the soul offers solace; when we wage inner battles, it emerges as our protector.

"The soul usually knows what to do to heal itself. The challenge is to silence the mind." - Caroline Myss

The soul's unique beauty lies in its unwavering acceptance of us, no matter how many times we may falter. Amidst countless missteps, when we finally seek to return, the soul's embrace is warm and forgiving, wrapping us in its reassuring hold. Such is the nobility of our soul.

We might betray our soul, deny it, refuse to accept it but still; the soul craves for us. In ways when we do not abide by human values like kindness, being truthful & helpful, humility etc. we betray our soul, yet it needs us and is one kind of our forever. It rejoices when we are happy and never abandons us. That soul loves and pampers us when we are alone and defends us when we are at war with ourselves. The beauty of our soul is that it accepts us no matter how many jargon times we betray it, still once we want to be back and submit to our soul, it hugs us tight.

Let us take it this way, if divide ourselves into two boxes. One house is the "Body Box," containing our ego, thoughts, pride, guilt, desires, pleasure, regret, selfishness, jealousy, and greed, while the other is the "Soul Box," our inner essence untouched by external chaos. It neither cares to worry about anything in the Universe or nor is there any filter or label applied on it. Initially, it is our Body Box which is at peace with Soul Box.

"The present moment is filled with joy and happiness. If you are attentive, you will see it." - Thich Nhat Hanh

As we traverse the journey of adolescence, a gradual chasm form. Overtime in life, as we grow into our teen life, the connection between

Body Box & Soul Box is raped and ripped off by the Body Box & the worldly desires. The Body Box gradually declines caring about the inner self or abiding by the Soul Box and moves towards controlling itself, who was initially in control of the Soul Box. The connection between them is eventually cut. How will there be peace if the Soul Box is jammed and choked by the Body Box? That is why we start feeling lonely & have a desire to feel complete as we do not feel so. The Body Box, influenced by worldly desires, strays from the Soul Box, severing their once-intertwined connection. This divide births loneliness, an insatiable yearning for wholeness.

Amid life's twists, our Soul Box continues to whisper instincts, offering glimpses of a future yet unseen. It acts as a mirror, reflecting truths we are not ready to see, a compass guiding us. But the chatter of the mind often drowns these whispers, leading the Body Box to dismiss the wisdom of the Soul Box.

You have all felt it – those times when something does not quite align, or you sense discomfort. These are the signals - the right calling, of the Soul Box, urging us to pause and reflect. The soul box knocks at us when you are wrong & celebrates us when we are right. Connecting and listening to one's own Soul Box was never a bummer. It signals," It just doesn't feel right" or "I don't feel good about this" this is when our Soul Box is signaling us, "stop, stop, stop." But what the Body Box does is, it denies all the signs from the Soul Box. Yet, too often, the Body Box ignores these cues, weakening the connection further. All the time the Body Box just denies, rejects, invalidates, ignores the Soul Box. Now, imagine about how ruined and thrashed the connect between the Body Box and Soul Box is. As the Body Box's ego and so-called witty choices keep increasing the internal connection with the Soul Box is halved and the gap keeps widening. Since, the Body Box and the Soul Box is now unfriended and there is no peace within, there are desires to connect, fulfill voids etc. An unbreakable connection becoming a distant memory. Driven by ego, the Body Box chases external pleasures, only to find fleeting fulfillment. Do you relate?

"Happiness is not something ready-made. It comes from your own actions." - Dalai Lama

Pop Your Bubbles

Next, the Body Box starts wandering around for peace, trying to find happiness in this material and external world, wherein encounters many more betrayals and ruins itself even more. After rigorous look out for peace, the Body Box gets tired and looks back, there is this Soul Box (our soul) awaiting our return, arms open wide. It whispers, **"At least now, come back my homie, my dear. My love for you knows no bounds."** Here is the marvel: our soul never deserts us; it is we who moved away. The wellspring of our peace, our Soul Box, beckons us to rekindle the bond. The journey requires shedding desires, releasing attachments, and embracing the soul's wisdom.

The day arrives when the two boxes harmonize anew. Here, peace and happiness interlace, creating a tapestry of bliss to share with the world. The source of our peace is the Soul Box, and we should try and heal our ruined connection with it. Slowly the existence of the Body Box (our acquaintances) should be eliminated, and it should merge with its soul, which is when there will be find peace and happiness; restored. We will experience the bliss and will be able to spread the same, because that is the home & peace, we are in search of. This is the homecoming we have always sought for.

If our soul is crying, body feels the depression.
If our soul is hurt, we will not be at ease.
If our soul smiles, we will be happy.
If our soul feels light, we will be on cloud nine.

As we rebuild this connection, loneliness fades. The yearning to fill voids diminishes, replaced by the understanding that contentment springs from within. To embrace solitude, we must first embrace our past, welcoming mistakes and voids without judgment. Healing stems from this acceptance. Bonds may come and go, but the bond with our soul is enduring – a companion through life's stages.

"Your task is not to seek for love, but merely to seek and find all the barriers within yourself that you have built against it." – Rumi

That lonely feeling, lingering desire to fulfill yourselves will always exist until you restore your soul connections. You need to refurbish and reestablish the connection, to attain peace within yourself. Only when you feel contented, you will feel the peace. To live alone, you need to learn to accept your past, the mistakes, and voids. You need to accept them to heal from them. This healing and acceptance are important because no bondage is forever, only the bond within you will last with you until the end. You are going to live only with yourself for the longest time. It's better if you understand this as early as possible.

Remember, your longest companionship is with yourself. The sooner you grasp this truth, the richer your journey becomes. Let yourself embark on the path of reconnection, where the fusion of Body Box and Soul Box transforms you into purveyors of tranquility, radiating peace to the world around you.

Actionable Insights: Recall a recent decision where you felt an inner unease. What were your instincts telling you? How did your Soul Box signal you? Jot down these insights and your response. Visualize how things might have unfolded had you embraced your soul's guidance. Use this reflection as a guide to align your Body Box and Soul Box moving forward. Your body and soul are tied, how you treat your soul will affect your body and vice versa. *Think! Because its interconnected.*

A Feast Of Words:

If you are depressed, you are living in the past.

If you are anxious, you are living in the future.

If you are at peace, you are living in the present.

EMBRACING HEALING WISDOM: INSIGHTS FROM WATER, TIME, AND BABIES

While you feel lost in the woods,

While you feel sorry for yourself,

While you feel helpless & hopeless,

Just be aware,

Of you & of water, and keep moving,

Of you & of time, and wait for none,

Of you & of a baby and live in the present.

And that change is a constant.

<u>*Quote says*</u>*:*

There are a bunch of learnings for life from all the stuffs around us, most importantly from the nature of water, time, and babies. Anytime, we feel overwhelmed or outbound in life, by just recalling these constant inspirations and we will be able to feel at ease. The problems or obstacles immediately will feel lighter, as you rewire your thoughts with these observations.

In the tapestry of life, physical pains receive immediate attention, while emotional wounds often languish unattended. It is as if we have a toolkit for mending cuts and scrapes yet lack the know-how to mend our bruised hearts. We do not have immediate doctors on pay as you go basis at our doors. Then we just start stacking all the emotional pains one after the other with the illusion of them being gone. But pains just do not go until you heal them, you need to treat them, you need to be on a sick off from the worldly desires while you heal from the emotional pain and work on medicating it. The good news is the nature of water, time and babies are forever remedies, these are like the paracetamol or pain killer for your emotional pain. Consider it soul medicine, a prescription for emotional well-being.

➜ Flowing like water - Adaptability and Resilience

Like water, we face obstacles which are alike stones in our river. But we must not shy away; instead, we need to navigate around or through them. Embrace Robert Frost's wisdom: **"The best way out is always through."** Challenges are our steppingstones, not barriers.

Water also teaches us hope and curiosity. Once settled, it seeks new horizons. Once it is adapted and comfortable in a space, it does not stop its growth, it looks for new opportunities and discovers its own new path. Bruce Lee's timeless advice rings true: **"Be water, my friend."** Cultivate hope, remain curious, and let life's journey unfold naturally.

Peace - like the tranquil surface of water, is our birthright. Amid chaos, maintain serenity. Water just stays at peace within itself, it does not care about the fellow beings passing nonchalant comments. Even if it is blocked with a pebble, it does not care because the water is detached and is at peace with itself. Be like water, untouched by tossed pebbles – let your inner calm reign supreme.

Be transparent like water, avoid carrying baggage of the past, be present in the moment without filters. Let your actions match your words.

→ **Flowing with Time: Consistency and Boundaries**

- Keep going like time - it never waits, it does not stop.
- Stay focused like time - it is not tempted by other distractions.
- Set boundaries like time - everyone has time, still they keep asking for it.
- Stay in control like time - it does not deviate for anyone.
- Add value to your life like time does our memories.
- Be detached like time - it is present for everyone but does not let their energies influence itself.
- Be regular like time - like it or not, show up every day.
- Be honest, like time - time never cheats.
- Be on time like time.
- With time, times' value is increasing.
- Steve Jobs said, "Your time is limited, don't waste it living someone else's life." Guard your time, it is the most precious asset.

→ **Embracing Innocence: The Wisdom of Babies**

- Babies, pure and authentic.
- Babies are innocent and straightforward. If they like it, they like it. If they do not, they do not. There is no misunderstanding & there is not in between, dilemmas like we have.
- Babies are present in the moment, they just live the moment to the fullest, they do not overthink or think ahead or behind time.
- Babies express their emotions up to how they know to, but they are expressive. They are happy they laugh; they are sad they cry.
- Babies do not fear anything, they just are curious to know and feel things. Einstein remarked, "The most important thing is to never stop questioning."
- Babies are honest.
- Babies live in the present. In Eckhart Tolle's words, "Realize deeply that the present moment is all you have."
- If they are hurt, they cry, they heal, they move on. They do not get stuck.

- There is a baby version in us, is craving a companion and that is why we love babies.
- Babies never give up on what they want. They cry and pester but never give up.
- Overtime, after coming through the mother, this little baby ruins itself and later wants to be a baby again. Life around us is here to teach us how to live, not just water, babies but everything else.

Actionable Insights: Pause, reflect on the analogies – water's adaptability, time's constancy, and the authenticity of babies. Write down three action points – adapting to challenges, safeguarding your time, embracing emotional honesty. Incorporate these steps into your daily life.

Life is full of analogies; we need to pay attention to learn from life. Water, time, and babies are some such gem-examples. It is what you pay your time to learn from. *Think! Because it's all interconnected.*

16.

DESIGNING YOUR CANVAS: CHOICES, DESIRES, AND TRUE SATISFACTION

Life will give you roses, lilies, sunflowers etc.

And will keep giving you more of it,

Life will give you heartbreaks, hurt, challenges, disappointments, etc.

And will keep giving you more of it,

Life will keep evolving & debugging,

It is all about how grounded we be,

It is all on you, on your choices.

It is all on what you accept to be yours.

Quote says:

The world will keep growing & there will be lot more which will come. There will be many more changes & multiple upgrades. It's about which path you choose and who you identify yourself to be.

In the theater of life, we are handed a script of choices, and the spotlight is on us to decide. As Helen Keller wisely noted, **"Life is either a daring adventure or nothing at all."** Picture this: Life's buffet spreads before us, from the finest delicacies to the not-so-appetizing dishes. We pick and choose, savoring some moments while grimacing at others. Just as Helen Keller's words remind us, we are the authors of our life's adventure, free to choose our path.

In this dance of decisions, the chase for the best can transform into insatiable greed, swallowing us whole. Life will always give us better to best & worse to worser and we need to choose what is good for us. If you are going to run behind this insatiability to always get the best or to always feel the least pain, the greed will swallow us. If you are consumed by an unending quest for perfection, you risk losing sight of the beauty in imperfection. As you run from discomfort, you may run into a maze with no way out where you might keep chasing for better to best. This voracious hunger pushes us but might lead us astray, causing us to exclaim, "You deserve more!" And in this chase, you join a herd of souls that drift aimlessly.

Any opportunity you get, it is because somewhere the Universe planned it for you, perhaps you deserve it and have the power to choose it. If you choose it, maybe, it will choose you too. That is where you will feel gratified. Every opportunity knocking on your door is a celestial dance of destiny. As Rumi whispered through time, **"What you seek is seeking you."** If you extend your hand, these opportunities might grasp it back. You want what you give, and you gave it because you wanted it back for you. While you do so, you are liable to expect what you share or give out, and what becomes mutual and is common in between is what is to be cherished. It is a two-way thing; you give and take. Nothing one-sided will work or make you happy in any way. It is about how less you are tempted to entitle yourself as "You deserve better," It is about how grounded you hold yourself and make a choice. It is all dependent on where you choose to hold on or put a break. It is about what you choose and what chooses you back. If you really deserve it, it will be yours. Just do not wait and mess in the mind for the best to happen, make it happen now.

Pop Your Bubbles

Amidst this cosmic dance, our emotional investments echo through time. We yearn for what we offer, planting seeds of hope in the soil of shared experiences. The threads of mutual satisfaction create a tapestry of connections, where giving and receiving form a symphony of emotions. Rather than blindly chanting "We deserve better," let us stand firm and grounded. As Maya Angelou once said, **"I can be changed by what happens to me, but I refuse to be reduced by it."** Our choices shape us, and we shape them in return. If a choice truly resonates, it will find its place in our lives.

Just like cherished friendships amidst the sea of strangers, it is vital to mend bonds that matter. As if echoing Maya Angelou's wisdom, **"Relationships are etched in memory through emotions, not transactions."** If we think they are worthy of us, do not let silly scuffs ruin it, hold onto to them, sort things out. Most importantly do not let them go if it is valuable to both of you. Two way is rare. Human connection is rare and gold. Quality human connections are like oxygen to the emotional part of us. If we lose these friends, the world is big, and its population is even bigger to make new friends. Millions of other people will come but none will be like these. We know that we can always get better options, and this is only valid for the materialistic choices. If it is a branded shirt now, there is a shirt of a better quality & brand always available. But when it comes to emotional satisfaction, we need to choose our satisfaction. We cannot keep updating our friend-list or partners just because we know we can find better options. On a material sight, we will get better in terms of quality and rest in the material will cause no harm to us. But in the case of humans and emotions while we get better humans, we will also be gifted with their traumas, emotional baggage's, past etc. The material and the emotional parts should be made with different mindset, and these are situational. Our brain synapses building castles in the air, to cue us to do more, feel more, want more, want new but we need to cut the crap and define our satisfaction. We need to understand how much is enough to satiate us and bind ourselves to it. The people in this world are all together working on never satisfying us and keeping us in the greed by updating every stream. Everyday there is growth in everyone's work and workflow. There is new development, discoveries, inventions, updates etc. everywhere and it is not in our control to stop it. **All we can control is our satisfaction.**

In our minds, a wizard conjures castles of desire. "More," it chants, urging us to seek, feel, and want; endlessly. But sometimes, it is essential to silence the wizard and define our own contentment. Amid the world's whirlwind of progress, our satisfaction becomes the North Star guiding us through the storm. Example, smartwatches with heart rate monitors, sleep trackers, and stress alerts. They are like modern sages predicting our needs. Yet not all of us require every feature. Just like wearing an analog watch, simplicity can be satisfying. By defining our version of fulfillment, we navigate through a sea of distractions with purpose. That is how we can define our type of satisfaction and stick to it. So, as we journey through life's buffet of choices, let us remember it is not just about choosing, but also cherishing. Embrace the dance of life's decisions, moving to your rhythm. And as the world evolves with each tick of the clock, let your heart's beat guide your steps.

Actionable Insights: Reflect on your recent choices. Are you embracing imperfections and the beauty they bring? Reach out to a friend you have lost touch with nurture connections that matter. Define your satisfaction and seek contentment within it. Just as you choose between the features of a smartwatch, decide what truly fulfills you emotionally and stick to it. **Your life is a dance choreographed by your heart's rhythm, not the world's noise.** If you keep stacking wishes, who will work on fulfilling them? Who sets the bar? You need to set the bar to feel that your particular wish is fulfilled. *Think, Because it is all interconnected.*

EMBRACING EMOTIONS: ADDING ZEST TO LIFE

Of those feelings,

Which are hard to deal with,

The hardest are regret & guilt.

<u>*Quote says:*</u>

Emotions like regret and guilt usually control us for long, they stay with us. This feeling arises when we commit a deed which is incorrect in our conscience. This thought about us being on the wrong side arises these disturbing emotions within us. We do not like feeling wrong about us and we end up feeling bad for the deed and the emotions risen out of it. These emotions are hard to deal with because neither do they let go of us and nor do we. They are like the leeches, once stuck unto us, they keep sucking our blood. It is a slow process to remove them.

Imagine life as a tall, cool glass of water. Now, envision emotions as those delightful syrups that infuse it with flavor. They are like the secret ingredients that honor us with feelings and make the ordinary extraordinary. Here is a secret: there are no inherently good or bad emotions. Emotions are chemical juices which add taste to plain water called life. Emotions honor us with feelings and make us feel alive. It is all about the mix of feelings that surge when those chemical reactions start to dance.

In this emotional orchestra, happiness releases a rush of dopamine, while sorrow might feel like an overflow of stress hormones. But remember, emotions are like fleeting guests at a party. They might linger too long, turning the party sour, or vanish too soon, leaving you craving their return. **Emotions are temporary**. We secrete excess or less of it, that is why we feel intense variations in the emotions. Emotions are of no value when the chemical is over in our body which lasts only for 9 seconds. If it is a happy or a dopamine, we get addicted to getting more of it. Emotions lose their sparkle once their chemical secretion fades within us. If it is the elixir of happiness, we become hooked on its taste, always yearning for more.

Love? Well, that is a potent concoction of dopamine and oxytocin, and we are drawn to it back and forth. But watch out, emotions have a cunning way of pushing our rational thoughts to the backseat, leading us to choices we might later regret and here is the thing: decisions made in the heat of strong emotions often fade out along with the feelings. It is like building a sandcastle – a masterpiece in the moment, but vulnerable once the tide comes in. We need to check on how the emotions are triggered like a touch releases oxytocin, eating favorite food releases dopamine etc. We need to allow the emotions to be secreted as they are and let them exist. But we must limit its effect on us. The trick is to find that delicate balance between allowing emotions to flow and not allowing them to sweep us away. We must direct on how much we allow ourselves to be gulped up by the emotion.

Now, let us delve into those emotion leeches – regret and guilt. They cling to us like shadows, subtly influencing our thoughts and actions. Regret is when expectations do not match the reality, the longing for a different past, while guilt is the sting of a mistake made. Sometimes, it is a tangled dance between wishing we had taken that leap and feeling remorse for the leaps we did take. We regret that we did not make a better call & we are guilty that we made a mistake and later regret it. Example: **We regret that we live & we are guilty that we did not live."** Isn't it this or the other, always? Familiar, right?

Here is the honest truth: **regretting decisions is like being caught in quicksand.** But guess what? Our past choices were right for us at the time, whether they blossomed or stumbled. Think of decisions as paintings – the true beauty unveils itself when we step back and admire the whole canvas. **Decisions are not etched in stone; they evolve over time.** If it was a wrong choice, we will learn or if it is right, congrats, we made it right. The decisions are not right or wrong, we make it right or wrong over time. Do not stress about deciding. When we feel out of our controls, just think, and respond; do not react promptly. Options come our way, because sometimes we need to see it, choose from it, or change our lives from there. We have life experiences over the years, we got that entire brain in our head and the gut feeling, just hit the notch with it. We are powerful enough to make a choice, embrace what feels right.

Life lays out multiple choices before us, but indecision often keeps us stuck. One part of us yells 'No!' due to unfamiliarity, while the other part urges us to seize the opportunity to avoid future regret. It is almost like these leeches are whispering doubts in our ears. But fear not. Prioritize, consider your bandwidth, and weigh the potential impact eventually. While such situations arise, just pick it up based on priorities and the bandwidth available to you. If your future self would look back with a smile, then go for it. At any point later in life, when you look back and regret at our call, just think your child version knew only this as the best way, that day.

Sure, your choice might reshape your world, for better or worse. **Regret or guilt is an emotional trap.** Regret and guilt come together & go together. These emotions are good until they help us drive life's choices, but they're bugs when they keep hanging around all life attached to certain instances, until lifetime. These emotions only can be rectified at the least. Yet, down the line, you will be content knowing that you made that decision based on who you were then. **Regret and guilt? Let us swap them for gratitude.** Embrace the challenges, the stumbles, and the quirky moments. They are the threads that weave your unique tapestry.

And guess what? In the years to come, you will be thanking the current version of yourself for them. Keep a dialogue of acceptance alive – "It's okay, it happened, no regrets now." Acceptance is the key to unlocking the leeches' grip. Train your mind to welcome this acceptance, to let go of the past's grip. Imagine autumn, gracefully shedding leaves without resistance. We, too, can learn to release the past, knowing that fresh chapters await us. If trees, with their silent wisdom, can release their leaves, surely, we can too. Accept. Release. Accept. Replace regret with the warm embrace of gratitude.

Actionable Insights: Try setting a daily reminder on your phone to jot down three things you are grateful for each evening. This simple practice can gradually reshape your perspective, moving you from regrets to gratitude. It is like seasoning your thoughts with positivity and savoring the richness it brings to your life.

If regret and guilt didn't exist, we wouldn't have the guilt of being inhumane or feel regretful on committing mistakes. It's a loop of goodness and badness and the key is to find the balance as *it's all interconnected.*

Pop Your Bubbles

A Feast Of Words:

All we do is anything but be grateful,

We be in favors and isn't it too much, overtime?

Gratitude is not only an emotion of respect,

Being grateful to changes and people,

You unload the sweet favors which you keep adding unto you,

Hence, be thankful of those, you will feel free.

You might hate this version of you,

Then why be thankful?

Be exultant that you are not worser,

Be happy that you fought death every day,

You tussled & brawled all your battles,

Both external & internal, alone,

Look around, people are going through worst,

And hang on,

Your best version is coming soon,

And I am sure you will love it.

TWO SIDES OF LOVE: ATTACHMENT'S EMBRACE AND DETACHMENT'S FREEDOM

Detachment is uncommitting,

It is being involved but untangled,

It is love and peace.

Attachment is committing,

It is being involved and swallowed.

It is a love trap.

<u>**Quote says:**</u>

While love is freedom, detachment is when we can feel the real essence of love. Attachment is falling in a tied commitment which is necessarily two-way, with dependent love.

Pop Your Bubbles

In the chain of human connection, attachment and detachment love emerge as two distinctive threads, each weaving its own intricate pattern. Imagine this: **Love as a bridge linking two souls, a bridge where needs, desires, and dreams converge.**

At the heart of attachment love, the yearning for completion thrives. It is the puzzle where our partner becomes the missing piece, the magic that fills voids we did not even know existed. But here lies the twist: we can only receive the love our partner possesses internally. Like Maya Angelou's wisdom, **"Love demands self-love too."**

Do you know why love demands self-love? Recall how in a newly wedded couple, the bride is able to accept the new family of the groom in her just married days. It's not because she is a saint, and she loves everyone equally. It's because the bride's love for the groom has extended to his family for the initial phases. **Likewise love demands self-love because that's the love you'll extend to your partner.** Love is somewhere an extension of existing love and is not newborn.

Likewise, is with mutual friends. Notice, how you can hang out with a set of new friends comfortably, just because you trust one of them. It's because of the extended trust of that one mutual friend which makes the group hangout, suitable.

(You may think the above paragraph is absurd but watch keenly **"Extension occurs in love."** *Or if you didn't catch my point, come back to me IG: @authorsaloni. Let's discuss. Now, move on!)*

→ <u>**Attachment:**</u>

Attachment love is a connection between two close humans. When there are needs and voids to be fulfilled by consuming someone which in-turn develops dependency for self-fulfillment, it is attachment. A person gives us love only if he or she has it. **In life, love cannot be borrowed and given, if that's the case then we are liable to return it, in such a transaction.** A person can only extend only whatever he or she has. Here, love is a bondage which we sign in the barter exchange, you give me love and I will give you love in return while on the inner side, both do not have love within to give. Isn't this a funny state? Picture love as a currency, unexchangeable and uniquely held. Attempting to trade borrowed love mirrors repaying debt with borrowed money. We find ourselves bound by the contract of love, promising it even when our own reserves run low. This is how our journey in attachment is.

When there is an attachment bond, it is bound to hurt, break & restrict. Attachment is when their happiness brings us joy and merriness. It is when they are in pain & agony that brings you pain and sadness as well. This is more than being sympathetic or empathetic. When someone is in pain? Should we help them or cry in their pain with them? To help them is our goal but the attachment makes us incapable of helping by replicating their emotions in us. It is when they cry, we cry as well. What is the point of both crying and not being able to help each other? Ah, the delicate balance of meeting expectations while staying true to our own desires. The weight of obligations often shapes us into compliant molds, altering our "yes" and "no" to match their desires. We feel liable to our partners expectations and if you do not fulfill them, the relationship becomes, toxic & unhealthy.

In this enmeshed version of love, we fall - but not just for each other. The phrase **"Jo Tera Hai Who Mera Hai, Jo Mera Hai Woh Tera Hai"** becomes our anthem. We feel tangled and less involved. Tangled is when we are tied by commitments, expectations, boundaries, duties, liabilities to fulfill our partners and mostly not being able to express self. The web tightens as commitments, expectations, and boundaries weave together, sometimes suffocating the essence of our true selves. The longing for freedom can conflict with the intricate threads of attachment, leading to a sense of confinement. All this might seem like love, but this is deceptive. **All this is what we have acquired as love overtime, but this is not love. ATTACHMENT IS NOT LOVE.**

→ **Detachment:**

Yet, a different path beckons - **that is detachment love.** It is a love adorned with healthy boundaries, where joy, care, and sharing appear much like attachment. The difference lies in the mutual support that flows between two independent pillars, no longer burdened with the task of 'completion.' Detachment love is a connection between two close humans where both the counterparts can be with each other by being themselves too. It is loving, being happy, blissful, joyous, sharing, caring, scuffing, enjoying etc. is not it looking like attachment? But detachment is more to this, it has healthy boundaries which both the party's respect. There is a healthy give and take transaction.

There are no expectations and hence hurting each other is rare. The partner is not liable to fulfill or complete the other. A relationship with boundaries will function well, imagine our partners over-boarding our boundaries, one day to life long. It will ruin our peace and the relationship as well. Detachment is infinite love with pure boundaries. Communication blossoms in this realm of detachment. Vulnerabilities, emotions, and weaknesses are openly and frequently aired. Boundaries serve as guardians, preventing the floodwaters of expectation from eroding the foundation of love. **Detachment evolves into a dance where strings are untied, replaced by the melodious harmony of shared feelings.** In this love we are detached but we engage in each other. We should be involved in love or anything we love to do, lest how will we live it fully unless we engage in it? We respect & feel worthy of each other. It is sharing of the love, which is already present within us.

Love is freedom & detachment but feeling connected. If a flower is pure love, freedom should be its fragrance. It is when their pain brings you grief but not sadness. That grief is being empathetic while our response to this situation will be more efficient, since our brain will function better, while our partners brain is down in pain. We will feel grief while they cry. We will be blissful looking at our partners happiness. We will be able to feel joy, not because they are also happy but because you are happy that they are happy, that is the blissful state. Here, we be in love with each other, and no one falls into each other. We share the love, feelings, emotions, wishes, thoughts, freedom etc. with complete comfort & there is meagre emotional dependency. When there is sharing and not pouring, there is hurt, break, restrict, liable. That is freedom and freedom is love. Here, **"Jo Tera Hai Woh Tera Hai, Jo Mera Hai Woh Mera Hai Aur Sab Apna Hai."** Meaning both be in each other's zone and at the end of the day we are there for each other. Partners flourish individually, intertwining from a space of abundance, not necessity. It feels like less connection with our partners but here we connect to ourselves and extend that pure connection to them, which is lovelier. It is in reality more & deeper connection.

(If attachment vs detachment is slipping over-head. It's okay! To understand these concepts, you need to go through that kind of an experience. Nevertheless, try the below analogy for better clarity.)

Imagine this detached love as water within two bottles. Each bottle is a partner, both self-contained and willing to share. The two bottles are detached from each other. The water in the bottle is contented when it is inside it is boundary (water bottle) and spills if the bottle is pricked. After the spillage, the spilled water is no more water which is consumable or contended, that is where the mess begins in a relationship. The contended feeling is when we are happy with ourselves and are happy to share our happiness with our partners. When people are in detached love, they feel peace and excitement out of self. The water rests contentedly within its boundaries, mirroring individuals who have found solace in self-acceptance. These individuals do not pour themselves into each other; they share from a well that overflows. Further to share between themselves, some water can be transferred to the other bottle when required and vice versa Yet, balance is key. Generosity and oversharing can overflow, rupturing boundaries just as water spills from a bottle's neck. That is when the actual boundaries are pricked in a bond and both the parties are in mess with self & each other. Imagine relationships like the two water bottles and perform the actions via learning & observing from it. Share thoughtfully, respecting limits. Just as the water preserves its essence within each bottle, let love flow without drowning individuality.

So, let this narrative of love guide you. There is love in any relationship not only between partners. Whether you are embraced by attachment or swept into detachment's dance, remember that love is the masterpiece woven from the threads of connection, comprehension, and shared joy.

(If it's still heavy on your head - close the book, calm down, and come back to it. I'm sure you'll be in a better state to grasp it. Otherwise, you can skip to the next topic.)

Actionable Insights: Reflect on your present relationships, pondering the harmony of attachment and detachment within them. Are there spaces where attachment's grip strains the bond? Can you foster healthier detachment by nurturing open conversations and honoring boundaries? Jot down your insights and craft tangible steps to cultivate more balanced and enriching connections.

We think we are attached and happy. But logically what in life is attached and free? Not even a rope is! Detachment has a stigmatic narrative of being saint-like. Being detached is allowing souls to be themselves and you being yourself. *Think! Because it's all interconnected.*

CHASING DREAMS, EMBRACING WONDER: A SYMPHONY OF EXPLORATION

Say, your goals are attained,

Say, you are at bliss with self,

Say, your love-life is settled.

Say, your financial problems are settled.

Say, you are happy with no problems.

Now what?

Just continue being curious,

Do not let the inner child, satisfy, or die.

Quote says:

We will reach our goals one day and find our happy family as well. At some later point, financial problems will be settled. You will be satisfied with your wants, beyond your needs as well. After we get whatever, we wished for, what comes next? It might be an idle, boring, routine state, right? What will you hold on to at that point in life? What will make your life worth living for? When you reach that idle state do not let yourself die, do not abandon your energies and curiosity. That will make your life amazing.

Pop Your Bubbles

In the beginning, a single goal seeds itself within us. Much like a tender sapling, we nurture it, providing the nourishment of determination and the sunlight of effort until it flourishes into reality. This journey, marked by overcoming obstacles, culminates in the victorious stand at our destination. Yet, as time flows, our focus shifts, dispersing towards various desires, needs, and wishes. Some become accomplishments, while others remain distant dreams. **If you grasp all, we risk slipping into the repetitive rhythm of routine.**

If everything is attained, we try to enjoy and settle the vibe and later it becomes monotonous. Amidst this whirlwind, the memories of how these pursuits once staved off emptiness and solitude can fade. Once we start to feel good daily with the least problems and no goals, we again feel that void, gap, or emptiness. **This disconnects manifests due to two potent reasons:**

1) The Cravings of the Inner Child: Do you recall the unbridled enthusiasm of your youth? That joyous spark within yearns for days of exploration and discovery. It pines for the thrill of recognition and the delight of embracing new experiences. As Robert Fulghum sagely observed, **"Don't worry that children never listen to you; worry that they are always watching you."**

2) Goals as Threads in the Tapestry: Goals became distractions that diverted our minds from emptiness, leading us to toil relentlessly in pursuit of dreams. In the words of Robert Brault, **"We are kept from our goal not by obstacles but by a clear path to a lesser goal."**

To bridge this chasm, we must weave together the threads of exploration and purpose. While we chase our dreams, we must remain anchored to our core. The disconnects can be fulfilled or repaired by keeping exploring, while working on our goals, we need to learn to stay connected to ourselves. **We need to know what are doing actually and what is the reason for it.** That is what spirituality holds. If we already be aware of yourself and the lives we live, we will be contended with self and will know what is to be happy like. We will not long for the goals to fill us or satisfy our needs. We will fulfill them ourselves.

Delving into the realm of spirituality, we uncover the 'why' behind our actions. This awareness births contentment, alleviating the need for goals to become our sole foundation. It is the rest earned after a day of balancing our inner chemistry. People sleep peacefully only when they are facing difficulties or problems. We go to bed peacefully because we know we have a reason to wake-up. Only when the inner child's urges are satisfied and there are imbalances and balances in our chemicals in the day, we get a blissful sleep at night, because our body did some workout, and it needs some rest. **"An empty mind will be a devil's workshop."** If people are only happy, or only sad, the blissful sleep will not show up.

When we attain all our goals, make sure we call out for new goals. Just do not sleep the life away. Be curious. Be a child. Be an enthusiast. Keep going better, day by day. Nurture an insatiable curiosity, akin to the spirit of youth. Progress step by step. Remember, the journey of exploration knows no bounds.

Actionable Insights: Pause and reflect on your voyage thus far. Embrace your inner child's curiosity wholeheartedly. Challenge yourself with this question: **"What new adventure or learning can I pursue today?"** Consider maintaining a journal to chronicle your daily reflections and feelings. Always remember, the path of self-discovery is an endless adventure *and it's all interconnected.*

CHANGING WORLDS WITH EVERY ANGLE: THE MAGIC OF PERCEPTION

Stories add value, life to things,

Stories make life worthwhile,

The stories we tell ourselves are the perceptions we have,

Perceptions are subjective, everyone has their own.

<u>**Quote says**</u>**:**

More important than what we do, the stories we tell ourselves are particularly important. Everything around us has a story to tell, because we understand from stories and stories add feelings/life to it.

Have you ever stared at a situation and thought, **"Is there more to this than what meets my eye?"** That is the enchanting world of perspectives, where we shape reality through our unique viewpoints. It is not just about how we see things; it is about how we choose to paint them. It is our form of a story which we tell us. **We dye our own colors.**

Picture perspectives as the paintbrushes of our minds. With every stroke, we create our own interpretation of the world. Like artists, we infuse life into the canvas of our experiences. Meet Sheela and Shreya. Sheela resides in luxury, craving even more money. Shreya, on the other hand is just well-off but treasures life's simple pleasures. Beyond material wealth, their hearts tell distinct stories – Sheela's heart yearns, while Shreya's heart overflows with contentment. Sheela has more money than Shreya, yet she is poor by heart, because of the story she tells herself and vice versa.

"Appearance is not the full story; the heart holds the chapters untold" – Unknown.

Consider there is a painting, which is not so attractive, when you know about the story behind it, you might end up buying it. A painting without a story has no value. A story gave it value. A tattoo without a story is simple pen and skin drawing. Stories inspire people. **We are so much moved by stories that we find stories as history in our books. "Art is a canvas; stories are its vibrant strokes."** - Art Critic

Beyond art, we are all storytellers. It does not end here; we tend to narrate stories to ourselves when needed. If a couple breaks-up on no reasonable terms, both will not be able to accept it because they do not have a story or reason to end it. They will begin to say stories to themselves, until they are able to make peace with the unexpected break-up. **These stories, like balm to wounds, guide us from pain to acceptance.** Through stories, hearts find their way home. Some stories like, may be, we were not meant to happen in this life. Stories can bring about change because it inspires through emotions. People's logical brain has only this or that scenarios while emotional brain process scenarios and helps us learn from it.

Pop Your Bubbles

Stories bring about change. It can make someone's day or ruin it. It is the sword for you. A good storyteller always has unfair advantage. Stories can heal, stories do rule. **We live in stories; we die in stories, and we are just a chapter from a story.**

"Words move mountains, but stories move souls." - Motivational Speaker

Stories can bring about a catastrophe, love, inspiration, power, courage, hope, experience, sympathy, happiness, energy, clarity, guidance, temptations, etc. every word I mentioned here, would have triggered a story in your mind, which is what stories do.

Our brain is an innocent organ, it is like a baby, it just wants what it wants but it does not want to put in efforts. It only keeps cribbing and we fall into the overthinking loop. It wants to sleep again even after you have slept for the whole night. It does not want to work, even if it idle. It just is so innocent that it wants to explore the world but does not want to earn for it. It is a super-lazy organ and always likes comfort zone. Now, think if you keep listening to brains commands, you will land nowhere. You need to narrate better commands to the brain, instead of it commanding on us. That is where stories come into play, you need to use your conscious mind to deliver such amazing stories to the brain non-stop, so that brain learns from it. That is the entire process of developing a habit, right? When you keep pushing the brain against its will on a consistent basis, habits happen. Do not listen to auto-commands of the brain, just take conscious efforts to command it & overpower it. This is important.

In olden days, people used to spoil other's stories in-order to revenge them. Now, to spoil someone's life or to avenge someone people tend to spoil the stories about them. Anyone will love to listen to a good public speaker, but everyone will learn from a good storyteller. Be a storyteller, express it in your way by writing, music, painting, etc.

With perceptions as our brushes and stories as our ink, we paint the canvas of our lives. Let your palette be vibrant, your stories compelling, and watch your life transform into a masterpiece of perception.

"In the end, we are all stories waiting to be told." - Unknown

And perceptions are important because they shape and tame our evolution. To find the ultimate truth we need to start with baby steps – Perceptions. If you do not start, how will you grow? Any perception about life will evolve after years. *Think, Because it's all interconnected.*

Actionable Insights: Pause and reflect on your perspectives. Are they enriching or constraining your experience?

- **Empathy**: Step into others' shoes. Embrace their viewpoints to enrich your understanding.

- **Narration**: Craft empowering tales. Transform negative scripts into positive affirmations.

- **Challenge**: Push your brain's comfort boundaries. This is where transformation blossoms.

- **Practice**: Practice the art of storytelling daily. Let your conscious tales sculpt your reality.

21.

EMBRACE THE DANCE: NAVIGATING THE WINDS OF CHANGE

Do we know ourselves?

Change & growth calls on us daily,

Every day we are a latest version,

How would we define ourselves?

<u>**Quote says**</u>**:**

We keep changing, growing, learning every day. Knowingly or unknowingly we just fix our bugs, or create new bugs, but we do not fail to update ourselves. Change is in a continuous tense. Can anything have a strict definition while it is in a process & it will keep changing?

Have you ever noticed your heart racing at the mere thought of change? It is like this mysterious performer is sneaking onto the stage of our lives, rearranging props while we are engrossed in the plot. But wait, change is not just a single grand showstopper; it is the gentle interludes that truly shape the story of our lives. **Change is a process; it happens daily, in insignificant amounts, with meagre effects.** We do not fear this type of change; we fear the jargon of many changes at once because it ruins our comfort zone. We are not afraid of those delicate shifts, the ones that tiptoe onto the scene; it is the dramatic entrance of transformation that sends an electric current through our emotions.

Let us break it down even further. Picture this: One day, you wake up feeling kind and gentle. The next day? Surprise, it is déjà vu; you are still kind. And guess what? The day after that, the pattern repeats. Now, fast forward a month, and a tinge of rudeness has stealthily made its way in. How did that happen? That change towards rudeness did not happen in one day; it took all these days of slow change, which is evident today. The change is like a gust of wind barging into our meticulously organized room of familiarity; it is that particular kind of change that keeps us awake at night. Change is like a skilled magician; it prefers long, subtle tricks. It is like the stream of a river gradually shifting its course until one day you realize the landscape has transformed. In essence, change is ongoing; we should accept changes as they flow and move on. So, why not cozy up to change? Picture it as that whimsical friend who quickly visits daily, bringing a new tale each time. Just as your day concludes with a verdict—was it good, bad, or just, okay? —you could apply the same lens to yourself. **Think of your life's journey as a continuously evolving painting, not just a series of isolated sketches.** Every day redefines the contours of your being, constructing a captivating, ever-changing image.

When you say, I am like this or that, your mind takes it as if it is right to be so. If you call yourself lazy, you slowly make it your identity, and you then become lazier to protect it. Without validating it as a weakness or a strength, you become stronger in what you identify as; later, you hardly want to change because you create a boundary, an ego, and an identity of your own. **We forget to grow there; it becomes a part of us.** This is the change about which we are talking. It is slowly bringing about a shift in your mentality, identity, and eventually you.

Hold on a second. Have you ever noticed how we tend to label ourselves? "I'm a patient person," you declare. But labels are akin to adhesive notes; they stick to our identities. Humans can go to any extent to protect their identities. If you label yourselves as patient, we will try to respond instead of reacting; we will tend to wait longer; we will just show yourselves to be patient; and you will stay calm in the storm just to protect our identity. If you label yourselves as calm, you might end up being calm with the rudest people and tend to allow toxicity in the name of kindness. Yet life is a spectrum of hues, not just a single shade. Consider identifying as kind yet struggling to assert yourself. We should not define or restrict ourselves in the name of kindness or any labels.

Ready for the plot twist? **Identities are not permanent tattoos; you are not etched in stone.** You are a kaleidoscope of ever-shifting patterns, not a static sculpture. Some labels might fit perfectly, like a tailored suit; those are worth keeping. As for the rest? Bid them farewell. These identities are boundaries; they restrict us from being someone else. Maybe a few identities are working fine for us in life, but those can be embraced while the rest are to be sorted at once. You are a symphony of contrasts, an artwork continuously unfolding. **Change is not an adversary; it is your dance partner, twirling alongside you in the grand ballroom of life.** So, take the time to understand yourself and cherish that inner child that is forever learning. Embrace the journey of revelation; your story is an ongoing masterpiece. **"The art of life is a constant readjustment to our surroundings.** Kakuzo Okakura. We are unpredictable; we do change, just as everything else does. That is what is meant by working on oneself: knowing oneself, self-love, self-care, etc. It means we need to educate ourselves because the inner child is an innocent soul.

Imagine, just for a moment, if you could take one label you have assigned yourself and tuck it into a box. Now, set that box aside. How does it feel? Liberating, isn't it? Remember, you are not defined by a solitary trait; you are an intricate tapestry woven from a myriad of experiences and emotions.

Actionable Insights: Begin a "Change Journal." Each day, jot down one minuscule change you have encountered – perhaps a fresh thought, a flicker in your mood, or even a taste of something new. Over time, you will witness the mosaic of changes that compose the symphony of your life. Through this, you will find yourself embracing the rhythm of transformation of other parts of your life too. *Think, Because it's all interconnected.*

22.

NAVIGATING THE EMOTIONAL LABYRINTH: FINDING BALANCE AMIDST THE CHAOS

Measure and recheck your moves while you are,

Extremely sad, depressed,

Extremely happy,

Extremely angry.

These extremities are getting you nowhere.

Moves in these extremities are mostly wrong choices.

Eliminate these extremities in the first place.

Quote says:

Do not feel extreme emotions because extremities ruin your capacity to think and respond, that is why you tend to react in extreme emotions. If you recall, countless amount of the decisions which you took in this highness would have led to guilt and regret.

Amidst the vivid tapestry of our emotions, Picture this: An extremely happy, sad, or angry state where we tend to secrete a high amount of respective chemicals. The secretion of the chemicals in normal amounts is sufficient for us to feel the emotion. Imagine a bewildered donkey, lost in its own emotional tempest, needing guidance to find its way. It is like a highly drunk human not in his senses and blurting things out. Since we cannot even keep a check on our senses, how would we be able to weigh what we utter when we are in such states?

Think of this as being in a realm of intoxication, where words tumble like leaves in the wind, unfiltered and unrestrained. This is why making decisions amidst emotional torrents is akin to catching a tempest with a net—it is a futile endeavor. In these moments, we are too engulfed to understand the threads of our thoughts, let alone weave them into coherent speech.

Think of yourself in cases like the following:

→ **Extreme Happiness:**

Consider those times when joy dances within you, leaving you breathless and exclaiming, **"I'm so elated, words escape me!** In that ecstatic whirlwind, your mind takes a brief sojourn from reality.

→ **Extreme Sadness:**

Now imagine the heavy weight of loss settling upon you, casting the world in shadows. When grief whispers, **"I'm shattered; hope is but a memory,"** your mind wanders deep into the labyrinth of sorrow.

→ **Extreme Anger:**

And oh, the roaring tempest of anger! A beast familiar to all, yet sometimes it slips its leash. Recall the moments when words spewed forth like wildfire, only to be followed by a sheepish **"I was furious; please forgive me."** In those moments, your mind temporarily surrenders to the storm.

Pop Your Bubbles

These emotions reign like monarchs to command our actions. But the key is moderation. Think of it as savoring a well-balanced meal where each flavor complements the next. Embrace your emotions, but do not let them seize your soul. **Balance, like a tightrope walker's skill, keeps your senses steady.**

Keep a check on the extreme emotions; they rule the world, they are based on you, and you are based on them. We need to feel the emotions, but not the extremities. **Just as ice cream delights but excess freezes joy, and lukewarm water quenches while boiling water burns, emotions demand a precise equilibrium**—a hint of heat, a touch of chill. Here lies the true essence of feelings, whether it is the shimmer of joy or the profundity of sorrow. So, let us embrace our roles as both actors and directors in this emotional theater. When joy knocks, sadness weeps, or anger flares, greet them with a knowing smile. In moderation and balance lies our truest selves, a masterpiece painted with the vibrant brushstrokes of emotions.

As a philosopher wisely said, **"True wisdom lies in the harmony of emotions."** Extremities are worthless.

Actionable Insights: In the grip of intense emotions, pause before reacting. Share your emotional experiences with trusted friends. Their insights can be invaluable. Engage in mindfulness exercises, like meditation. Keep a journal to track emotional patterns. Identify triggers and strategies for control from other emotions. *Think, Because it's all interconnected.*

PHYSICAL EXPERIENCES: THE WISDOM OF BRUISES AND BUMPS

Learning from experiences,

Creating biases from experiences,

Both are mirror reflections of each other.

This affects us for a lifetime,

Take the first and leave the latter.

Quote says:

While you experience a past trauma or go through some negative phase, may it be physically, mentally, or emotionally, we create biases in our mind. We create a cause-effect map in our mind, the next time when we are triggered by a similar cause, we fetch the bias of the effect and act accordingly.

Pop Your Bubbles

Picture life as a captivating tapestry woven from three distinctive threads: the physical, the mental, and the emotional. Each thread carries its own hue, contributing to the vibrant masterpiece of our existence. Let us move in a journey through these threads, unveiling the insights they hold.

Physical Experiences: The Wisdom of Bruises and Bumps

In physical experiences, it is normal to go through some hurt. We learn from it and make sure we do not repeat it because we do not want to face that pain again. Imagine a curious baby encountering boiling water for the first time. In that moment, scorching pain becomes a guiding light. This tiny explorer learns that actions have consequences as the sting of the hot water shapes its future interactions. This physical lesson illustrates how experience forms the bedrock of our understanding. But problems arise when we apply the same learning to our mental and emotional experiences.

Mental and Emotional Experiences: The Art of Learning and Unlearning

In emotional and mental experiences, learning should be ceaseless, and biases should be created only after patterns because every human is unique. Biases should not be created immediately. More than trusting the cues or gut, you need to trust patterns because the gut feeling comes from our experiences and not from theirs. As we venture into the labyrinth of mental and emotional landscapes, we encounter a realm where learning should be a ceaseless pursuit. Biases should only crystallize after patterns have emerged. Humans, like snowflakes, possess their own intricate patterns. Rushing to judge based on immediate cues robs us of the rich tapestry of individuality.

Think of it this way: An old friend's betrayal instills a bias against trust in your mind. But projecting this bias onto new friendships is akin to passing on an old wound. When you share your bias, you unintentionally cast a shadow on others ability to build deep connections.

Consider another scenario: A friend radiates kindness, yet your biases cast doubt on their sincerity. By yielding to biases, you unwittingly sabotage connections. Similarly, love's vulnerability can be eclipsed by past traumas, preventing the blossoming of genuine affection.

Now, picture emotional lessons as subjects in a classroom. Just as math and science evolve with each grade, our understanding of emotions should grow with each experience. No two humans will ever give us similar experiences. Humans are never-ending learners. If it did not work in the past, maybe it can this time. Let the emotional pain be until experiences and not trauma. It is not that the physical experience with which we touch hot water or fire today will feel different tomorrow. It is going to feel hot all the time. The hot water is not unique every day, but with emotional humans, the experience is not hot (an effect of experience) all the time; it changes from human to human. Every person we encounter pens a unique chapter in our life's book. Let us savor these chapters, allowing patterns to guide our perceptions rather than hastily formed biases.

Say your remarkably close friend cheated you in the past, and that learning is etched in your mind as a trauma or a bias. In your present and future, if you make friendships, will you be able to reach a close bond? Because you have created bias or trauma from the past, you will not be able to build deep relationships. Now, the new friend of yours will have to go through pain that is like what you went through because of you, since the new friend will be trying to build a good relationship with you, and you will not be reciprocating the same with him or her. The new friend has no history of bias in friendships. Here, you gave your trauma to someone else and invalidated their capacity or confidence to build deep or good relationships.

Recently, a friend of mine was being genuinely sweet and nice to me, but the biases that I had in my mind were triggering me to say, "How can someone be so nice and sweet? The moment the bias or trauma was triggered, I ruined the connection between us. I gave her the bias, "Being nice is bad," for none of her mistakes. I have also been fracturing my ability and opportunity to build human connections. That is not how it should be, right? I recall one more scenario from my life, where a friend of mine was genuinely in love with a guy and was ready to put in efforts to work it out. She felt he would be a good match for her and was going head over heels for him. At that time, she did not know about his past bias towards not trusting anyone. She was putting in efforts consistently, and at the same pace, he was going emotionally away from her, and eventually everything ended. It is not that he did not want to trust her; he tried, but his emotional experiences and trauma made him choose the latter, to be safe.

Emotional maturity is to be open to learning and subjective, as we learn updated science, math, etc. in every grade of our educational life. Likewise, we need to look at new experiences in a fresh way and be open. Every human is a new subject or an updated subject. Running away from these will take us nowhere; we are bound to face and be them. Of course, this is not giving you a degree on a piece of paper; it is giving you a learning for a lifetime, on people skills. Make sure of the pattern-related cues and react accordingly. Be open; life has so much more for you. It is high time that we realize that it is important to heal from all the impressions and trauma we have. Only after healing from the existing biases will, we be able to embrace life for its purpose and feel detached. Healing is the balm for biased hearts and wounded souls. Acknowledging and mending biases empowers us to embrace life fully, detached yet passionately engaged. Detachment, paradoxically, fosters the purest form of attachment. It allows us to dance through life's opportunities without old shadows tarnishing the brilliance.

Remember, this is not a diploma to hang on a wall; it is a lifelong skill. People, connections, and life itself are the canvas. Paint it with patterns, not prejudices, and witness the colors intensify as the connections deepen. Your journey now radiates wisdom, depth, and a profound sense of fulfilment.

"The past cannot be changed. The future is not yet in your power." — Unknown

Actionable Insights: Identify a bias stemming from past experiences. Reflect on its influence on your perceptions and interactions. Challenge yourself to view situations and people anew, guided by patterns rather than snap judgments. Slowly weave this practice into your daily life and watch out for its side effects too, *because it's all interconnected.*

A Feast Of Words:

We go through divergent phases,

We start analyzing them,

We create conclusions based on what we think is the cause,

These biases get swollen overtime,

Later, when similar situations arise,

These biases pop-up like an alert screen,

We hold back, out of the fear of pain,

We then miss being exposed to a different phase,

It might not be a negative one,

Yet we fear.

Do not apply one learning too all.

Do not apply all learning to one.

Have it as a one-on-one mapping.

LEARNING FROM EMOTIONAL LESSONS: A LIFELONG CURRICULUM

Be you, be authentic, Be original,

Be yourself, Be your edition,

Present yourself,

Not the one, which the world validates.

The moment you be you,

You will love your insecurities.

Quote Says:

Present your own self, not the one which the world will please, love, accept or validate. Be that version of self which you offer to validate and accept. That is when you will love your inner self for being real. Because real is safe, authentic, rich.

Life's journey begins as a precious gift waiting to be unwrapped. Yet, the path to authenticity often withers away unless a guiding hand shows us the way. Authenticity is showing, being, walking, talking, and doing who you actually are effortlessly. No filters, no lies, no faking, no hiding, etc. Imagine a world where authenticity is nurtured from the start, shaped by mentors and parents alike. As we navigate life's stages, growth takes on a symphonic quality: **physical development occurs until age 7, emotions take the lead until age 16, and then mental faculties flourish.** It is as if biology laid the foundation for our psychological masterpiece. However, this canvas is still stretching and evolving, painted by experiences. We step onto life's stage, facing societal expectations while our emotional selves rehearse and learn by the side.

We tend to face the world while our emotional brain is growing; at that point, only validation, acceptance, pleasing, love, importance, and self-value exist. Self-esteem does not come into play at that age. While we face all this pressure that is put forth by the world, we tend to fold and squeeze ourselves. By the end of the day, we need someone to whom we feel safe and who we can fall back on. Unless we have the right mentor, we cannot be ourselves. From childhood, being authentic is out of the book already.

Picture a world where authenticity is not a lesson learned late, but a guiding principle cherished from the outset. This is the call resonating within—an invitation to dance to your own rhythm, prioritize your uniqueness, and revel in your essence. Later in life, when we understand that being authentic is good, it is too late. So, I bring this to you: **To learn to be yourself, prioritize yourself, and embrace yourself.** Practice this.

Let me share a personal story: A walk with my friend Rohan. Curious about his strengths and weaknesses, I asked, and he described attributes foreign to his being. Bewildered, I watched as he presented a version of himself that contradicted his essence. Going deeper, he admitted, frustration coloring his words: "I don't know who I want to be or what resonates with me. In that moment, authenticity's vital role struck me. That is how we will remember ourselves; otherwise, because of worldly validations, we will only remember what the world sees us as. If you do not become who you are now, the layers that the world paints all over us will last permanently, and we will not be able to see ourselves ever again. The wiring in the mind will get stronger and harder; it will reach a state where it cannot be undone later, and we will forget ourselves forever. The more we delay being authentic, the more we are disconnected from ourselves, and that is not a good place to be. The more disconnected we feel, the more our self-esteem is ruined, and the more we will be far from peace, which lies in connecting to ourselves.

Imagine mentors as stars, steering us towards authenticity's compass. They navigate us from imitation to individuality. That was him, who came into my life and reminded me to be myself, and that was a game changer. Later, I started accepting my flaws and working on the wrong ones. This insight urged me to embrace imperfections, whittle rough edges, and transform flaws into strengths. Yes, it takes time; it is challenging but worth the effort to feel at peace with oneself. So, fix your mistakes, be your true self, and know this - **that is what the world needs, and that is what the world should accept.** This journey is demanding, like refining a sculpture into art. Each step is significant—a stroke in the masterpiece of our lives.

Ever noticed how we deceive ourselves while deceiving others? While we fake to others, we fake to ourselves as well, sometimes we fake to others and sometimes we fake to ourselves. It is a complex dance, adopting virtues we lack like costumes for a performance. We become skilled actors, mimicking others, or crafting personas. This skillful performance muffles our true calling. Ironically, our quest for peace sows' turmoil, disconnecting us from authenticity.

We tend to fall blindly to the virtues we do not have, more easily. We then try and take after those. We work on replicating someone else or a combination of many others perfectly, repeatedly. It disrupts our actual desires, peace, and nature. We long for peace of mind, peace of heart and peace in life whilst we ourselves ruin it, what an irony, isn't it? All through this, we start missing ourselves, we create a new form of us with a completely different biodata. Thereafter, we begin to hate ourselves because we have always denied our inner calling. We feel lost and disconnected to self and others as we fake, we will gather only unreal companions which obviously do not last longer.

Actionable Insights: Embarking on self-discovery requires action. Stand before a mirror, gazing into your eyes. Reflect on the day: "Have I embraced my authentic self? Have I celebrated my uniqueness?" This exercise reinforces authenticity's value, reminding you to stay true in all situations both to self and to others. *Think, Because it's all interconnected.*

A Feast Of Words:

Our fears force us to be someone else,

Makes us fake our moves,

You know,

It requires two times efforts to be like someone else.

Practice being real.

While being real, we will know where we stand, what we are.

While being unreal, we will find hard to spot ourselves in the crowd,

And that is the worst that can happen to us & ourselves.

Do not be your type of you, be you.

Say "It's just how I am."

Perhaps, people love the real you, more than the "Someone else" you.

MENTORS AND SELF-DISCOVERY: GUIDING LIGHTS ON THE PATH TO AUTHENTICITY

As hearts shatter,

We create love out of those shattered hearts,

With all the bits and pieces together,

We give more love than before.

We learn to love, even more.

And the beauty to the eye is,

The way humans hold each other to make each other happy,

With all the bits of broken heart.

Doesn't this spark a ray of hope?

Quote Says:

There is pain, heart break, hopelessness, and void everywhere but the way humans pull themselves out of it and still wear a smile has its beauty and is commendable.

Imagine a rainy day when a stranger's warm smile brightens your spirit, or the story of Mr. Thompson, who mows his elderly neighbor's lawn out of pure kindness. These moments are not just heartwarming; they are a testament to the profound power of kindness. As Maya Angelou wisely said, **"The more you know life, the more kindness you instill."**

Like the intricate notes of a symphony, kindness weaves its melody into the fabric of our actions and intentions. Just as beauty is in the eye of the beholder, every gesture we make holds the potential for kindness. Mahatma Gandhi's words echo: **"You must be the change you wish to see in the world."** For a kind person, kindness is not only from himself, but from the world as well.

Being kind is a journey, and to develop it, one must feel lifelessness and hopelessness. It takes a toll on all the losses in our life, all the painful phases we have, overcoming all the prejudices in life, all the lows more than the ups, all the falls, all the loveless days, the lonely ones, and all the heartbreaks. Because only then do we learn its value and importance. Thereafter, we learn to admire even the bits and pieces of life; even the smallest moments become worthy of recall. We do not learn its value until we lose it or live without it. Every act of kindness is like a thread woven into creating compassion and empathy. Remember Leo Buscaglia's words: **"Too often we underestimate the power of a touch, a smile, a kind word."**

Once kindness takes root within, it becomes an inseparable part of who you are. It guides your actions and choices, making unkindness feel like a betrayal of your essence. This essence guides you even when the path is challenging.

Kindness is not a solitary virtue. It is a sync of all the other values; it has some patience or may be a lot as well; a lot of care; anger the least; some humanity; more optimism; and a sincere desire to give without expecting anything in return. Kindness is more about giving than taking. Perhaps that's why kindness is tougher to instill. It is an ongoing process. Dalai Lama XIV's words hold true: **"Be kind whenever possible. It is always possible."**

Pop Your Bubbles

Imagine yourself as a gardener, tending to the delicate plant of kindness within your heart. As you nurture its growth, it blossoms and spreads its roots, transforming not only you but the world around you as well.

Action Insights: As you embark on this journey, imagine recording acts of kindness in a journal. Capture the impact these moments have on you and others. As you set forth on this journey, remember that your actions, like drops in an ocean, can create a ripple effect that shapes a brighter tomorrow.

A Feast Of Words:

Everyone out here is hurt and is shattered,

We are all trying to maneuver our trashes,

We say "Shit happens" but what next?

We do not give up, we do lose hope, but we raise back,

We still muster the energy to love our loved ones,

We still hold on to that weary smile,

And that is the beauty here.

Not that we are faking it,

Not that we must wear a smile after pain,

But that is how our hearts are!

Perhaps, that is how we spread a word of hope,

Perhaps, only a broken heart can teach the art of love.

Perhaps, only a broken soul can reside kindness and love for the world.

26.

FROM PATTERNS TO POSSIBILITIES: NAVIGATING YOUR JOURNEY WITHIN

You are living on auto-mode on patterns,

Everything we speak is because of a pattern,

Every deed is a pattern,

Recognize the patterns,

Understand the patterns,

Reason out the patterns,

Break the wrong ones,

Keep the right ones.

Quote Says:

Everything we do is a part of the web in our minds. It is a pattern which has trigger points and its effect points. It has a start and an end point. We have a lot of patterns in us. We react, behave, talk, joke, think based on it. We need to segregate the traumatic patterns and rewire them.

We live in a dual world, there is duality everywhere. A dance between our inner whispers and the voices of the world around us. Among these echoes, our true self yearns for expression, while societal murmurs seek to shape us. Often, we lend more weight to the chorus outside than to the melody within, which overshadows authenticity and leads to the creation of subjective patterns.

Personal Patterns:

We tend to subside our own feelings and modify ourselves according to the world. When we try to function based on the dual world and fake to ourselves, we create a masked version of ourselves within us. These masks are formed because we create patterns in ourselves which is a byproduct of our thoughts or the thoughts which the world pushes into us.

When you are born, you have zero patterns, you do not know anything & react to nothing apart from living in the present and sleeping. Slowly patterns are taught to you. A baby touches the boiling water and learns to shoo hands away. This happens 2-3 times and it creates a pattern in its mind. This is on an innocent level, a pattern which is created by an external world. As you grow, anything you learn; is framed as a pattern in your mind. When you asked your mother to buy you, your favorite toy, or junk food and she denied the first time – a pattern started forming. You kept coercing her and still she didn't budge. You rolled out tears and eventually you got it. This on repetition 2-3 times, created synapses (biological reference) in your brain - a blueprint for emotional manipulation emerged. This was on a partial emotional level, a pattern you created for yourself, that if you want to get something, you have to coerce with tears. You have to keep pestering and, in the end, you win. Earlier, this pattern was just to own a toy/food but as you mature, patterns evolve into complex emotions. Later, it is more about the fear of losing or feeling considered or validated.

Let's venture into the world of relationships, where patterns converge, intertwine, and sometimes clash. Imagine courting a crush, driven by a childhood pattern—perhaps a longing for the favorite toy in the past and now to own a cherished human. This triggers the old relevant pattern, and the mind says, **"I know what to do, that's a pattern match."** Next, you will put in some efforts because you are on a better maturity in life. than earlier. If the pattern is not satisfied yet, you will start coercing or keep trying until you get them. Just because you created a pattern from years, which says you will eventually get it, somehow. Uneducated of the fact, that sometimes you cannot own them or owning them was never in your life's game. You just learn that you should own what you want, not that the other person's interest matters. It is how you wired your brain. These patterns impel you to persevere, fueled by the belief that your desires will ultimately bow to your will.

For instance, if it still does not work out, you will start an alternate pattern to look for someone else who will consider you or will be easily ownable, because that will satisfy your pattern. While you keep coercing the crush, you are also in clash with the other person's patterns. Perhaps, that person was taught to not own something in a compromise or may it be some other learning. Remarkably, patterns are not immutable. They can splinter or transform under the right conditions. When two patterns converge, they might harmonize or spark metamorphosis. Consider the habit of saying "Yes" when "No" beckons. It originates from a pattern of seeking approval, yet it can be rewired. When two patterns merge, there are patterns which can break, or new and better ones can be formed.

These patterns mature and migrate, extending their influence into every facet of our existence. Notice how we utter "Yes" while meaning "No"? This stems from a pattern woven with a desire to please, trading authenticity for external approval.

Pop Your Bubbles

Is it that we wear heels, to stand out or to grab attention or to look attractive or do we feel good wearing those pencil heels? Most probably it is the fear of neglected and fear of invalidation in the fashion world. Who wants to walk on that needle with the fear of stumbling upon somewhere?

Let us take one more scenario, a teacher keeps teaching all day or night without any boundaries for self. She keeps her brain intact all the time and explaining stuffs until she is really exhausted, because that will make her feel worthy and helpful and wanted in the society. Whilst her inner calling asks her to just take some rest, be there for self, have boundaries, she denies and still teaches. Since she is extremely available, it also means that she might be a people pleaser and will be taken for granted. This is a pattern which needs to be broken & replaced. Let's see how she navigates through her pattern:

➔ Old Pattern:

- "What's the reason for my exhaustion?" - it is overt teaching.

- "Why do I over-teach?" - because I like teaching.

- "I like teaching and not over-teaching, then why do I do so?" - because I feel worthy and considered in the society although my heart wants to rest.

➔ Breaking the Pattern:

- "Why am I declining my hearts' call?" - to feel validated in the worldly patterns.

- "Should I not break this now?" - yes, I should set boundaries to what I do and take rest now & then. Making sure I do it just because I like it and not for the sake of validation.

Boom, she tackled it. That is how you need to observe your patterns, you create, or the world creates for you. The more you observe your pattern, you will know what you are looking for and what you do around it. That is when you will know how hollow your thoughts are and how wrongly programmed, you are. **This is the easiest way to know your weaknesses and the reasons for the same.** While you observe the trigger and the effect, also check where did you create that pattern first. Mostly all patterns are from childhood and are very strongly wired, as hard as a diamond. **That is why self-work and self-awareness is important.**

Any pattern which denies the inner calling or the inner voice, is to be broken and changed or erased or replaced. Introspecting the actual reason behind the pattern, look for, where it is coming from - is it from fear or abundance, void or need, passion or validation, joy, or consideration, loneliness or companionship, love or jealousy, hatred, or neglect, value, or ignorance, attention, or importance etc. Mostly these patterns are because of some kind of a fear. There are very less patterns which come direct out of the inner calling are smoothly doing its impact and causing its effects.

That is why, it is important to be flexible, because only then you can tweak your existing unhealthy patterns and form new ones. The people who are rigid and do not stop until they fulfill their patterns, are the ones who are stuck in life. Have you come across some people who just would not try to understand your point of view and claim to be right always? I am speaking about them. They cannot accept novel changes and patterns. You cannot put forth your opinion or convince them because they cannot build a new story in mind or create a different pattern. They are really tough be around with.

Relationships Patterns:

Even relationships are choreographed by patterns. The key lies in mutual awareness, in understanding not only your patterns but your partner's as well. Relationship is when two people join in hands and invest in each other emotionally. Here, they are invested with their past & present patterns. They carry their baggage along with them. When the two patterns are not soluble in the relationship, the patterns can be rewired or changed. Suppose one of the partners crave for reassurance in words, the other just expresses it in the care, there is a pattern mismatch, but it can be worked out to make sense of it. Unfortunately, people don't realize that this is more about collaboration and that these patterns can be rewired, if the partners wholeheartedly allow it. To make this worse, people in a relationship are unaware, that they are in a web of patterns. People stick onto what they think will make them happy or sad, energized or validated, included, or excluded. They just do not realize that it is not how they are, it is changeable, instead they call it to be their identity. Instead of modifying the patterns, they adapt to it, sink with it, dive deeper into it, such that they identify themselves with it. Identifying ourselves with any pattern, value, label, or titles, is the last thing we should ever do.

Before getting into a relationship, be aware of your emotions and patterns. It will help you understand why you act a certain way, in a particular scenario. It will make life easy for you because when you are aware of yourself, you will automatically extend this awareness in the other persons' behavior as well. You both will begin to act from a conscious level. You as a couple, will realize what is wrong and what is to be changed. More than half of the complexities in the mind will be washed away because you will realize that those were not in your range of control and were not a problem from your end. Best way to begin to be aware is by meditating, slowly and steadily. Then we do not even have to look for patterns we can just stay, the patterns will unleash themselves. Life will be a lot easier. Relationships will be a lot better.

Relationships are the source of most of the problems, "**Expectations**" in a relationship are the major problem. As we know that, we yell out in anger sometimes because we feel insecure and unsafe about someone which is a pattern from our childhood, the other partner might also be likewise. Once we realize and be aware of ourselves, we begin to understand ourselves and as a result we understand the other as well. All this applies to all sorts of bonds, friendships, marriages, sororities etc. Wherever there is emotional investment, this will happen. Before two people invest themselves into each other, they are expected to go inwards to work out oneself, checking on the baggage which each of them carries, from their childhood. The partners who think are compatible with each-other, should work on this because it will take the relationships to better level and restore peace & happiness. If being aware is feeling like a struggle and after a lot of trails and errors, you as a couple are not getting better, seek advice, seek help, seek therapy & counselling. But just do not commit to each other before committing and understanding oneself, because you will be carrying over everything and enforcing it, unto each other.

Parenting patterns:

Parenting is also a relationship. Imagine forcing our patterns unto our innocent kids. The unaware parents work-out their own relationship somehow to have kids and then be like the so-called happy family which is now complete, because they are going to make their kid the best in the world, as they themselves could not be the best in their lifetime. All the opportunities they lacked in their own life are suddenly so important that, they want their kid to experience those opportunities. They will push and pull the kid towards it. In all of this, the kid is not being raised but used as a tool by them to fulfill their desires and dreams. The kid is only grinded and not brought-up or raised. Because of the enforcing patterns, the kid does not realize that he might be capable of something else, anytime. The kids are molded via their patterns. If we consider a scenario that parents can fulfill their past voids via their kid, how does it make sense that the kid will be excellent in whatever they did not get to experience, after-all the kid is a byproduct of their traits. Isn't that a blunder and injustice to the kids' unexplored skills, talents, and the kid, himself? Eventually, it would look like an inanimate object, a robot being petted whose remote is with the parents. The kid is likely to be like you and what you want it to be. This will only disconnect the kid from oneself.

The parenting mindset needs to be changed. The initial step towards the change is that parents should think that the kid does not belong to them. Yes! They have given birth but holding onto it will only bind the kid to the parents tightly, day by day. This will lead to influencing the kids' natural aroma, simply because, you think you own it. The parents should become aware that the kid is creating new patterns, and most importantly, they should heal from theirs.' This will help them be conscious parent who will then help raise a kid and not maneuver themselves towards the kid, as if the kid belonged to them.

After being aware, the kid must be raised as the plants are raised. While we raise a plant, we sow the seeds, provide it with all the necessary nutrition, and allow the plant to grow on its own. We do not tell the plant that it should bend this much only, that it should not only give flowers but fruits as well. It should give blue instead of red flowers. We just allow it to be and let it grow on its own, so that it can give its best results. We make sure that we keep track of the growth pattern, avoid unhealthy insects, the weeds and use a scarecrow for their safety. Just so that the plant can grow on its own pace in the best environment. Similar is parenting, it is not growing child, it is raising a being. It is not about holding onto the kid, with the title "my kid," "my child," "my love," etc. It is about teaching the kid to realize himself, his inner self, and embrace his capabilities. Not labelling him as per the norms of society, just letting him feel and be himself. Like the plant is irrigated only how much is needed, giving it the best possible environment. That is the base from which parenting should begin, without instantly creating patterns and boasting your dreams as his. Taking care of the kid, being there for the kid, not always when the kid requires it—is parenting. Liberation begins with recognizing these patterns. Instead of scripting a child's destiny, become a gardener, nurturing their unique essence. Let the child flourish, unhindered by parental desires.

Actionable Insights: Take time to introspect and recognize recurring patterns in your behavior. Dig deep into the origins of these patterns. Identify their source—fear, validation, or other factors. Choose a pattern for transformation. Draft both the old and new narratives. Actively practice your new pattern. When triggered by the old pattern, recall the new narrative. If patterns resist change, seek advice from professionals. Remember, seeking help is a stride toward growth.

Every pattern you got, expresses itself in whichever absurd situation it matches with. Pattern unfolds itself even when you think you're being conscious of it. Even relationship pattern might express itself in absence of any relationship. Patterns are basic programmed logic to which situations are inputs and outputs are the current version of ourselves. *Think! Because it's all interconnected.*

27.

BEYOND THE CLICHÉ: THE POWER OF POSITIVE EXPECTATIONS IN RELATIONSHIPS

Expectations are good to some extent,

Good expectations, add smoothness & flavor to bonds,

Good expectations are a sign of trust.

Whilst bad expectations just ruin the bonds.

There is a thin line between good and bad expectations.

Quote says:

Expectations are both good and bad (excess) and that they are a sign of trust. Whilst everyone says, "Don't expect anything from anyone." Expectations are healthy up to a balanced level for any bond to sustain. It sets a benchmark in the relationship.

The well-worn advice, **"Expect nothing and you won't be disappointed,"** rings in your ears. But here is a secret twist: not all expectations are villains in the story of relationships. Amid the cautionary tales, they forgot to mention that certain expectations can actually be the threads that weave bonds stronger.

Let us dive in, shall we? We are always told to expect nothing out of anyone because we are awfully bad at setting and living up to expectations. While it is wise not to tether your happiness solely to someone else's actions, let us not toss the whole idea of expecting out the window. When we are emotionally invested and genuinely care, expectations sneak into the room like confetti at a celebration.

The Good Expectations Formula: **Good Expectation = (Capability + Interest)** or Reality, which is like calculative expectations. Picture expecting a fish to swim—that is reasonable. But are you hoping it will sprout wings and fly? That is where the line blurs. Trust your gut to sort the doable from the dreamy expectations. It is akin to expecting a plant to thrive when watered, not when given a gourmet meal.

Let us talk about expectations as emotional transactions. It is like a trust-based barter system not that relationships are transactional. Expectations are a result of your investment in a bond and are directly proportional in which one side of expectation is replaced with money. You invest your emotions, and in return, you expect certain responses. It is a pact sealed with trust, where you count on the vendor to deliver the goods. We can estimate, based on our insights, how much can be expected from the other person. Also, notice that if you want chocolate, you pay the exact amount for it, not less or more. This is for the growth of both parties. This barter is one form of expectation, which on an emotional level is **termed "Emotional Expectation."** In a bond, you invest yourself emotionally; you give the brittle parts of yourself to the other person. Why is the expectation in that place wrong? Expectations are a sign of emotional trust between both parties. Expectations are a two-way passage, like a transaction, and are for the sake of the connection between the two. They hurt only when it is a one-way process. **Expect the obvious; expect the doable; such expectations will never disappoint us.**

Pop Your Bubbles

Bad expectations also include the tiniest things in a relationship, like expecting an extrovert to be an introvert or expecting more care as an expression of love from a person who expresses love via romance and cuddles. Every human has their own expression of feelings and personality type. Identify what they are capable of and will love to engage in, because fulfilling expectations is not only about you but also about the other person, enjoying fulfilling it.

But hold on—your happiness? That is your responsibility. Expecting someone else to be your eternal joy factory is like asking a penguin to give calculus lessons. While you expect, you need to keep in mind that only you can fulfill yourselves. You are not to expect that the other person will make you happy, joyful, satisfied, complete, loved, etc. Happiness is to be expected of yourselves. Do not try to extract emotions from the other human; keep expectations that enhance the connection between the two. The rest of the fulfillment and satisfaction must come only from yourself.

Let us get practical. **Expectations should be like a flexible yoga pose, not a rigid stance.** Consider them guidelines, not rigid rules. Do not be so strict about the expectations you set, let them be flexible and non-chalet. Let the doer, feel no pressure to fulfil them. Anything under pressure will not be out of love. Let the bird fly its own way and be back. If your partner surprises you with breakfast in bed, do not engrave it in stone and expect it, next day too. Life evolves, and circumstances shift. Talk openly, understand, and let the harmony continue. When patterns emerge, like your partner's morning coffee ritual, keep the communication lines wide open. Nobody is flawless, after all. So, if the coffee routine skips a beat, converse and unearth the "why."

Imagine if people in a relationship just kept working on self-improvement, self-love, self-care, etc. What would happen to the bond or connection between them? Would it not wither over time? To make relationships work, it requires both parties' contribution, it takes two hands to clap. **"Anything that is not irrigated or nurtured, will not grow."** If you stop irrigating the water plants, indoors, won't they die? You need to constantly rear and foster them. Likewise, in relationships, the expectations are to be nurtured, but you set the wrong expectations and ruin the bonds instead. Setting good expectations to enhance the relationship will help cherish the connection.

What should I expect from someone? - "Do not assume; communicate about what the needs are." Like we explain to the vendor what we want when we pay, why is it that we do not communicate expectations to our partner? Expectations require proper communication. Usually, it is not that we expect it, but that we expect it and do not communicate about it. Suppose it is your girlfriend's favorite ice cream bar. If you are just going to visit that place to get some work done, the girlfriend will start expecting that you will get her an ice cream on your way back. She assumes but does not communicate it. Maybe you will also go for another chore nearby and return late. If your girlfriend communicates about her need for ice cream, you might get it, or if it is not possible, you can explain it to her, so that her mouth does not drip for the ice cream. Probably make a statement like, "Will you get me an ice cream while coming back?" These are small acts of love that add to the vibe of the connections. Communicating expectation makes things clear, shows the feasibility, also makes the person who expects feel important. It makes our partner feel validated and needed. These are the desires which we always want to feel from our loved ones. Only a highly spiritual person will be contended, devoid of this.

Set the right expectations - Set the request, where you are sure the partner can deliver it. Not to expect a fish to fly or a dog to swim. Set the expectations based on capacities. This will help you move smoothly ahead in life. This mostly concerns the individuals' love language. Like in the scenario mentioned before - she might expect reassurance from her partner as per her need, to feel safe in love. He might have all the gentle caressing gestures, as his love language. So, he will tend to show more care to her, because he thinks that is love, and she will try to give you reassurance, because that, in her mind, is love and she expresses the same. *(Read the previous line 2 times, slowly. Make sure you get it right)* But here, both are not expressing love; instead, they are expressing what they want. The expectations here are not set right and are blindly uncommunicated.

Pop Your Bubbles

To resolve this, both can talk it out to each other and collaboratively fulfill the expectation in a way which enhances their bond. They can work on each other's perspective of love and show results, respectively. If there is no collaborative conclusion, then a re-check on the connection is demanded, because love is all about the little doable compromises here and there too. For someone we love, we should not mind tweaking ourselves to a bit. Setting the right expectations will not hurt, because now you know which ones will be fulfilled and which will not and in turn this will restore peace and satisfaction.

Believe in action words because efforts matter. In case you communicate about a trip you want to go with your partner, perhaps, your partner might not even want to visit that place but makes some efforts to make it happen or makes it collaborative for a trip to some other location which even interests him, isn't it a win-win? Notice the minor changes towards meeting your expectations, in terms of actions. Because here it is about, sacrificing ones' desires for you. **Actions towards fulfilling expectations are way more significant.** Do not imagine all the expectations to be fulfilled, most of them, will not be. That is why you can rely on the actions and the efforts taken, which itself is an attempt to be fulfilling.

When it becomes a habit, people expect more: When some gesture is played on a regular basis, we tend to fall into it, eventually. Say your partner makes you coffee every morning, it will be an expected gesture out of her. It is now a pattern and when this breaks, because it was an expectation, it hurts. We can still talk it out, it helps.

Actionable Insights: Envision a garden – your relationships are delicate blooms. Nurture them with care, bathe them in understanding, and let the sunlight of communication grace them. Watch your garden flourish. Know that the petals of expectations can add fragrance to your journey.

If you create expectations from your partner which doesn't fit into any of his patterns, he sure is going to disappoint you. *Think! Because it's all interconnected.*

UNVEILING THE EMOTIONAL KALEIDOSCOPE: A JOURNEY BEYOND LABELS

Like a thirsty bird finds - water,

It is not joy but a quench.

Like a farmer finally gets - pouring rains,

It is not a gift but satisfaction.

Like a rat finds its - way home,

It is not success but safety.

Like a cocoon finds its - way to fly,

It is not freedom but life.

Like a storm finds its - calm,

Its safety for you but loss of self for the storm.

<u>**Quote says:**</u>

Often, we tend to swap and assume our feelings. We generalize every positive emotion as happiness and every negative emotion as sad. But is that the right way to deal with the emotional situations?

Pop Your Bubbles

Every glimmer of joy is not a mirror of happiness, just as not every shadow of sorrow spells desolation. Life is not a binary interplay of happy and sad. The renowned psychologist, Carl Jung, once wisely remarked, **"Even a happy life cannot be without a measure of darkness, and the word 'happy' would lose its meaning if it were not balanced by sadness."**

As the sun casts varied shades on the landscape, emotions too morph and shift, responding to the winds of circumstance. Not every good feeling is happiness. Sometimes it is about connection, productivity, or satisfaction, not every sad feeling is a desolation. Similarly, longing for a dear presence or yearning for more is not just sorrow; it is an emotion that demands its own recognition. Emotions are not limited to the dichotomy of happy and sad; they are an intricate mesh, woven by the threads of circumstance.

About emotions, we often leap to conclusions, hastily labeling what we feel. Yet, the grandeur of human emotion extends beyond this limited lexicon. We frequently tend to switch between assumptions of feelings, any low vibrational emotional state leads us to label it as sadness because that is the most appropriate, we know. But the truth is entirely different from what we know from our experience. Sometimes we go to a state of nameless feelings & emotions, speechless thoughts, confused words, insecure surroundings, and involuntary moves too. This is a state of uncertainty in the unknown. **A new network of emotions.**

Within this enigmatic realm, emotions take forms beyond our known vocabulary—nameless feelings, indescribable sentiments. Thoughts escape words, surroundings turn uncertain, actions become involuntary.

Philosopher Alan Watts invites us **to dance with change, to move with it, to join its rhythm.** Why then do we rush to label, to confine the unknown to the known? Why not let the unknown feeling be unknown? Labelling offers solace to the anxious mind, a sense of belonging in the tribe of normalcy. Once low vibe is named sad, brain knows that this is a known feeling. This is how brain tricks you into thinking however it wants to. That is why it is important to take in charge, dictate the brain. Picture an emotion that is not purely sad or happy, but a fusion, a dance between the two. Imagine a circumstance where you are feeling good about missing someone as SAD. This is not a completely sad or a happy emotion. It is a mixture of the two or in between. Accept, while you are feeling different, unique, anew, colorful, dissimilar. Tell your brain unknown is good too as true growth lies in challenging this compulsion.

Any change or shift in emotions brings about a horizon of emotional and mental transformation. Sometimes it might look like you are fighting with yourself, and other times like you are befriending yourself.

It is an odd, complex journey. That emotional experience is not the older feeling. It is uncertain and cannot be labelled. If this is not okay, then life should have been predictable. Why is life so unpredictable then?

Actionable Insights: The next time you feel an emotion, pause. Do not rush to label it. Instead, let it flow, observe it like a masterpiece in progress. Ask, **"What shades does this emotion carry? What message does it hold?"** As you do this, you will find liberation from the confines of known emotions. Embrace the spectrum, let the unknown wash over you. The true beauty of life lies in its unpredictability.

Emotions create labels which in turn create stigmas/biases which will further trigger some existing patterns. That's why it's important to be hugely self-aware. *Think! Because it's all interconnected.*

FINDING HARMONY IN EVERY MOMENT

You see a bird; you want to fly.

You listen to songs; you want to listen more.

You read a delightful book; you never want to end it.

You write a poem; you want to write one more.

You are happy now; you look out for the same joy again.

Did you ever watch a bird for its own nature of being, flying, nesting etc.?

Why is it that a bird is supposed be of our use & fly for us?

Did you listen to a good song and not want to listen to it once again?

Why is it that we want to escape from us with anything good we find?

Quote says:

Anything we like or do is in some way an escape from the reality. While we are doing something, we are escaping millions of other things. "Doing" is an effort and we put in efforts when we either want to get benefits or not want something else. Alike, while saying a YES, we say NO to the rest. While we do so, we keep working in the name of efforts and misinterpret it with living life. We are escaping reality in the name of the "Doing" rigorously. Every day we are doing a lot of things, but effortless doing is life and effortless doing is just being in the moment. Just to observe it as it is and not to interpret or analyze with efforts which only ruins the truth or the reality. Thinking and judging the observations only brings you far away from the truth or reality of it because judging is filtering with one's own experiences. – *Read again.*

Amid the clutches of sadness, our hearts yearn for happiness, if we are sad about someone's presence around us, we want to just get away from there. There are times when shadows linger, urging us to seek refuge in solitude. Boredom and restlessness engage in a playful waltz, wanting to fidget and minds to wander. A question beckons here: Why do we unfailingly saturate our moments with ceaseless activity? Whenever you try to pursue something, you go with a horse-eyed view. Isn't it an escape from the rest? It is good in terms of dedication and discipline but what about living reality and life. What about experiencing humanity and life? There should always be a balance. A balance will always enhance the speed of growth.

You watch a lovely flower; you want to see more such.

You are watching the moon; you want to see the stars also.

Imagine gazing at a delicate flower, its petals whispering secrets to the breeze. In that fleeting moment, it is not merely a flower; it is an entire Universe contained within that fragile beauty. Just watch a flower for its beauty and liveliness rather than taking it home or switch the beauty to another flower. Let not everything be about yourself and your happiness which is an egocentric attitude. What about the flower's life then? It will die once you pluck it, that is self-centric. Likewise, is for the moons and stars. The moon graces your gaze, and your heart extends its reach to embrace the stars. A craving for experiences blossoms. Yet, before you follow that celestial path, remember the first flower. It deserves your undivided presence.

Instead of having the book to never end, you need to read it for just how beautifully articulated it is, just for reading and learning than wanting it to last forever. **Won't it be selfish of you to want the story to never end, just because you are enjoying it?** You are not only hindering yourself from a lot of better days or phases, you are escaping life in the name of pursuing it but also getting into ties and stuck. You must make peace with the fact that life will change, and phases will end. Try not to escape life in the name of poem, art, beauty, happiness, or anything itself. **Can you try to be happy or sad without knowing that it will fade away?**

Pop Your Bubbles

Life flows like a river, its currents weaving change into its very fabric. Phases wax and wane, akin to the moon's journey across the night sky. Embrace You are escaping yourself, in all the forms of art, music, books etc. Why is everything only about you? Why did we make everything about ourselves? Why are we escaping ourselves with wanting for more of everything else? Why did we use a fantasy to escape reality? Why is no art looked at without us as a filter? It was not supposed to be this way. Art was not supposed to bring us far from ourselves, it was not.

And then, there's art, music, books—the realms where we often seek refuge. Yet, let us reverse the paradigm. **When did we become the central force of every encounter?** Art was not meant to distance us from our core; it was crafted to mirror the depths of our souls.

As you journey onward, remember: **"Life is not about waiting for the storm to pass, but about learning to dance in the rain."** - Vivian Greene. As pages turn, in both the chronicles of books and the epic of life, recall this truth: The allure lies in each chapter, each moment, and each connection, making the entire tapestry truly extraordinary.

Actionable Insights: Be present, fully absorbed in your surroundings. Feel the breeze on your skin, savor the flavors in your meal, and really listen when someone speaks. Notice the intricate details that often go unnoticed. Embrace the moment without thoughts of what comes next. By practicing this mindful presence, you will unwrap the gift of being alive in every instant, nurturing the dance of life within you. **"The present moment is a powerful goddess."** - Johann Wolfgang von Goethe.

While past and future thoughts seem to create more complexity in life, we got to stay in the present. Being aware of the present always is just like being meditative always. *Think! Because it's all interconnected.*

THE ART OF LIVING FULLY: NAVIGATING LIFE'S EVER-FLOWING RIVER

Why forever and forevermore?

Were you happy at ends,

For the new starts, at least?

Were you imbibing the now,

For what the present offered, at least?

Did you allow happy moments to slip away,

Happily?

<u>**Quote says**</u>**:**

You always seek forever in everything you do because of the certainties about it. If you like a food, you want to keep eating it daily. You keep looking for repetition of your comfort zones, you want to get back to them iteratively. You eventually start hating ends which are beautiful as well. You are celebrated at starts and while the journey commences and when the end is near, you feel dejected because you were never taught to rejoice ends. If you start it, it will end someday, and we must know this.

Pop Your Bubbles

Yearning for that joyful flutter again and again? Who would not! Longing for those fleeting moments to stretch out into eternity. Ah, if only. But alas, reality softly reminds us - **the clock ticks, and moments, they are as slippery as mercury.** While we want to feel good feelings repeatedly. We want moments to last forever which is practically and emotionally not possible. Imagine a life where happiness unfurls ceaselessly, like a never-ending dance party. Sounds like a dream, right? But it is going to be boring and perhaps ironically, you will start wanting sadness. Imagine being served the same dish over and over. The spice, the thrill, the excitement – they would vanish like a magician's trick. Funny how even joy can become routine. Tell me, is there anyone, just anyone, who is missed the rendezvous with sadness, joy, elation, heartbreak, love – the whole emotional rollercoaster? Not likely. Life is like this extravagant thali. A bit of everything is sprinkled on it – joy, sorrow, sweet, spicy. **It is not just yours; it is shared with the world, too.**

Imagine that thali in front of you. You get your slice of cake. Sweet, right? Yours to consume whenever you choose. But remember, one slice is all you get. The rest? Is reserved for others thali. So, eat the sweet now or save it for later – your call. Just like that sweet slice, every phase melts away. But here is the kicker – that is what makes this thali truly delectable. A never-ending buffet of experiences, waiting for you to explore, savor, and devour. A bite of sadness here, a dollop of joy there – it is all in the mix.

Now, picture life as a book. You flip its pages, eager to unveil what is next. Sometimes, you get a surprise gift – a laugh, a victory. Other times, you hit a speed bump – a tear, a trial. Guess what? It is okay. The pages keep turning, the story keeps unfolding. LIFE is, likewise, keep flipping moments but do live them. The only way to stay stuck is by not flipping. Not flipping pages means, getting stuck, not knowing the reality, being fearful of ends, not living it fully. Imagine reading just one page, forever, oblivious to the grand saga.

Keep moving on, do not linger on the same page for it to last forever, just because it feels good now. Embrace the flow of life, is it not beautiful to think what next moment could offer?

Life, my friend, is also like a TV channel with endless shows. Keep flicking through, but for goodness' sake, watch them. Feel them. Do not freeze on a frame, hoping it will never fade. Instead, flow with life's current. Isn't it exciting, not knowing what the next scene brings?

"How dull life would be if it were just rainbows and no rain." - Unknown

Now, how many fairy tale endings have you seen? Each ending's a fresh prologue, each beginning has its own goodbye. A common notion - **"It's ending, let's be sad."** Try flipping that script. **"Why not cheer for the ending?"** Celebrate the joy, or yes, even the ache. They are all chapters in your life's book. Learn, grow, feel. **"Endings are the palette from which new beginnings are painted."**

Remember, each experience is a golden ticket to life's amusement park. Others are in line, craving their turns. Do not swipe away your chance. **Embrace the ups, the downs, and the loops.** Do not lock the infinite life in a finite box. You are not caged. Life is not a fish gasping for air. Let each moment flow, like birds set free. **Yes, there might be falls, but hey, what if you soar?**

Actionable Insights: Write down three lessons or insights you gain from reflection on any life experience, positive or challenging, that has contributed to your growth. Just like flipping through pages, embrace life and make a commitment to carry forward these lessons with you.

Life and your karma have a planned end for you, why try to go reverse on the law? Start to enjoy the randomness of life. That's all it has, don't try to analyze and belt a philosophy around everything. This is too much thought into life, sometimes life wants to take a break from you too. *Think! Because it's all interconnected.*

YOUR LIFE, YOUR CANVAS: PAINTING A JOURNEY FREE FROM COMPARISONS

You are doubting yourself,

But your friend is not feeling skeptical because of you.

Every story, yours or mine is inspiring.

Every one of you is an inspiration.

Believe in the magic inside you,

Believe in the magic that you are.

Quote says:

You often tend to underestimate or overestimate yourself. We start counting our behavior in comparison with others. If someone is better or less good, you underestimate or overestimate yourself, respectively. Humans are unique and meant to be so. Humans can learn about life and relationships majorly via relationships or people because people are the source of emotions, brain, knowledge, and wisdom. But what your takeaway in the form learning from those comparisons is what matters.

In the magnificent mosaic of life, comparisons often masquerade as captivating illusions. Picture this: You're an acrobat on life's tightrope, teetering between two extremes. On one end, you are inflating someone else's journey as the epitome of success. On the other, you are shrinking yourself into a shadow, letting doubts have the stage.

But let us untangle this web of comparisons. These illusions, you see, are not the compass to self-improvement; rather, they are like the extra baggage you lug while ascending the mountain of life. They are the fog that distorts your vision, rather than the lighthouse guiding your way. In comparisons, when you overestimate yourself, you are creating false confidence and while you underestimate you are letting insecurities into yourself. Comparing & rating yourself is no way helping you be a better human; it is making life tougher to navigate for you.

Every comparison is a trade-off. A piece of your authentic self for the borrowed identity of another. Imagine exchanging your unique melody for a tune that does not resonate with your soul. When you compare, it is like snipping petals from one bloom and grafting them onto another. The moment you compare you want to be like or unlike the other person which is not possible in life. A human is not capable of being exactly like the other, that's not life's law. A human can only learn or absorb and implement in ones' own candid way which is going to be different in every sense.

Who rates, estimates, or give marks? An evaluator or a teacher who is an expert in their profession. Are you? or the people around you experts in skills to estimate oneself? or is rating your profession? Why do you have to complicate your own life with wrong estimates? In matters of self-worth, who is the authority? Are you an expert on your intricacies? It is like seeking a chef's advice on architecture. It is time to shed the burden of misguided comparisons.

Estimating your capabilities or capacities out of comparison is not what you should learn rather learn about how much any human is capable of, what's the magic unique to every other person, admiring how people grow and embrace change, being a complementary support to each other is what you need to carry with you.

Pop Your Bubbles

In comparisons, you are not only judging others but also yourself, what else can be sicker about comparisons? You are capable of doing everything you wish to, just practice and the relevant intention to put efforts is what is important. Now, let us twist the kaleidoscope. You are a creator, a dream weaver. **The recipe for your magic potion?** Diligent practice fused with unwavering intent. Acknowledge the boundless potential within every human—a potential that cannot be bottled into someone else's measures.

Comparisons cast a shadow not only on others but also on your own brilliance. It is a loop that thrives on self-critique and external evaluation. But here is the twist: you are the storyteller, and you can rewrite the narrative.

Pause when you find yourself sizing up another's journey. Instead of analyzing theirs, celebrate their unique voyage. Through this, you will immerse yourself in the kaleidoscope of your capabilities. For, your potential is an artwork unlike any other.

Remember, dear reader, you are the conductor of your life's symphony. With every note, you compose a melody that is yours alone. Bid adieu to the symphony of comparisons and let your personal melody soar. **"Comparison is the thief of joy."** – Theodore Roosevelt. Consider Picasso and van Gogh—both were exceptional painters, but each carved his distinct path.

Actionable Insights:

Practice Pause and Praise (PPP): When caught in comparisons, pause and praise both yourself and the person you compared yourself to. Shift focus from comparison to celebration. If you start celebrating others, you will celebrate yourself too. **"The more you focus on the good, the more it happens to you."** *Think! Because it's all interconnected.*

Saloni S Jain

A Feast Of Words:

You are enjoying, living, and creating life in you.
While someone is asking GOD, "Why Me?
You say, "Thanks for choosing me."
You are not resistive of the events in life,
You are just accepting that life has no strings attached.
While you are questioning your moves,
Someone else is relying on your moves.
How much of magic you reflect, how could you doubt yourself, sweetheart?

EMBRACING THE PAST: HOW CHILDHOOD SHAPES OUR NOTION OF HOME

Any phase which helps you grow the most,

Any phase you are most emotionally invested,

Any phase which helped you learn about yourself a lot,

Any phase in which your innocence was washed away a bit,

Would always be lingering in your heart.

That phase was your home, for once.

You felt safe there.

That is why we always love to go back to our childhood,

That is why we always love our school friends.

Quote says:

The phases in which we are invested most of the while are hard to move on from, that stay etched in your heart and that is why it is hard to move on or get away. It can be any phase, good or bad or any toxic phase.

The place where we grow from our childhood becomes our idea of home and peace forever in life, unless you heal. May it be in the arms of the babysitter or in the remotest village with the fewest possible amenities. That is the stage when we start from scratch and our body gets wired. These are the moments that set the stage for the masterpiece of our lives. They etch our earliest impressions of home, shaping our perceptions in ways we might never fully grasp. That is when we build our emotional connections for the very first time. We feel touch, emotions, care, and love while we grow daily. The nature of living within the boundaries of the home becomes your idea of lifestyle, and day by day it gets stronger in the mind and later shift to the subconscious mind. We need to be incredibly careful about the environment that a kid develops in because that phase has effects later in life.

Now, let us unravel the remarkable secret of these early impressions: They are not just fleeting imprints but indelible marks. Like echoes reverberating through time, the environments of our youth continue to influence us in ways that might surprise us, forever. These influences become the lenses through which we view the world, coloring everything we see.

Pause for a moment and ponder: How does this shape our reality? How does it mold the connections we form as we journey through life? These questions lead us to a critical juncture: the crossroads of emotional investment. When we open the door to connect with others, we step into uncharted territory. It is like setting foot in an enchanted forest where the path is not always clear. Every time we put ourselves emotionally into someone or something, we will come out as changed.

In this journey of connection, the possibilities are endless. When it is right, it is like walking through a garden where the fragrance of trust fills the air, and cautionary signs are rare. But when it is wrong, those signs flap urgently in the wind, urging us to reevaluate. Imagine stepping into someone else's world, pouring your heart into it. But what if that world is a labyrinth of toxicity? What if the love you invest begins to warp your understanding of what love should be? It is akin to gazing into a hall of mirrors, where the reflections can distort reality. The longer you remain, the more this distorted perception becomes familiar, eroding the solid ground you once stood on.

Consider this: Each connection you form, each bond you weave, changes you. It is like taking brushstrokes from another artist and adding them to your canvas. Choose wisely, for the people you invite into your life can reshape the masterpiece you have been creating. They can introduce new colors or muddy the waters. It is a dance of vulnerability, where the steps you take can lead to growth or heartache.

So, here is a thought to carry with you: Amidst the tapestry of life's connections, remember that your early perceptions, your first notions of home and love, matter. They are not relics of the past; they are the building blocks of your present and future. That is why childhood experiences are important, they shape the way we will respond to future life circumstances. Reflect on the connections you have woven. Are they amplifying your understanding of love, or are they distorting it? Any first time experience you go through, may it be the first ever date, first ever coffee, tasting a new cuisine, dancing on stage for the first time, trying a new hobby, partying for first time, reading a new book, trying a new sport, cooking your first meal etc. creates a strong GOOD or BAD experience within you around it, just because it is for the **"FIRST TIME"**. Never have you ever tried it and that's why it is etched deeply. It is important to enjoy the experience and not get attached to it, because if the experience is good, you'll re-do; if not, you would want to escape it, always. Of all experiences, our first-time moments – are associated with our childhood as everything we do had a start, somewhere in the childhood.

I remember going out for water sports for the first time and some mishap at the sport gave me the fear of water. That's why first timers are the rule makers for you. Remember to set the right rules. Take a moment each day to recall a positive or negative childhood memory, letting it remind you of the foundation on which you stand. Try to understand if it is just because of the first time or that you really do or don't enjoy the experience. Nurture the connections that uplift you, that water the roots of your understanding, and gently weed out those that sow toxicity.

In life, remember that you are the conductor, directing the melodies that play within you. Each chord struck, each connection formed, resonates beyond what meets the eye. Your perception of love, of home, of the world—it's a masterpiece still in progress, waiting for your brushstrokes to shape it into something beautiful.

A Feast Of Words:

This too shall pass, all we have is now,

Aren't these controversial in itself?

We are told to live in now, also told to think about the future,

Where is the present?

We are told everything shall pass, also told to make now beautiful.

How to?

We make promises for forever, although we know,

Forever is a myth.

We are told to forget the past, also told to plan the future,

Where is the present?

We are told to love; also told not to hurt the ones we love.

How to?

We are told to live the happiness,

We are told to learn from struggles,

Also told nothing is permanent.

We are told to hustle and told to celebrate every moment.

The answer to the "How to" (s)?

Is to find a balance.

Life does not work in extremes, baby.

Balance is important.

DISCOVERING POETRY IN LIFE'S EVERYDAY MOMENTS

What you feel, speaks your story,

Perhaps what I feel may be the latter,

And all this speaks about what you seek and do not,

Listen to what your poetry sounds like.

<u>*Quotes says:*</u>

Imagine a lyric without any orchestra, just reading words and they make sense. Likewise, life is meaningful in however unpredictable it is, but there is no rhythm or taal and the beauty is that poetry adds to life like orchestra does to the lyrics to make it worth longing. That is why, everyone seeks poetry and life is a poem, a music without rhythm, a clap of various unions. Each of you have a unique poem about yourself and that is what is rhythm to you.

In life, where every note carries its own unique melody, we yearn to discover poetry in the simplest of moments. Picture this: A quiet afternoon, the sun's gentle caress, and the aroma of fresh coffee filling the air. It is in this everyday scene that we find the first verse of our personal poem. As Robert Frost wisely observed, **'In three words, I can sum up everything I've learned about life: it goes on.'** As every poem has its own language and is understood in ambiguous ways by all of us, everyone seeks poetry in whatever they aspire to seek or be. We uncover poetry in the folds of our favorite hobbies and passions. Any favorite trip, book, toy, bike, car, moment, song, food, movie, series, person of yours is a poem and will definitely tell you a poem about yourself. That is why you love it, and it stays with you.

As you listen to a friend passionately talk about their dreams or recount their adventures, that moment the world takes a pause for us and starts revolving around them. Maya Angelou reminds us that **'people will forget what you said, people will forget what you did, but people will never forget how you made them feel.'** How such human of an insignificant size in this Universe can cater about conquering their dream. How is this moment lesser than a poetry?

We all seek to both feel and not feel the emotions we bare. We seek it and that is what is magnetic about all of us. This magnetic pull towards the profound is what poetry does to our souls. See, how you are able to trek mountains for that view, echoing John Muir's call, 'The mountains are calling, and I must go.' How you go to that party for you seek freedom and happiness, how you listen to a song just for that one line, how you go miles to re-taste that food, how you re-watch a series to laugh again, how you re-visit your gallery to feel that moment, again, how you go back to Instagram to escape life's confusions, how you get back to that blanket, to feel comfortable, how you wear red to feel loved, how you go back to that person, to feel secure, how you get the stars and moon, to see that smile of your love. Just see. FOR ONCE, JUST SEE. That is where your poetry lies for you and that is the orchestra you add to your life.

Pop Your Bubbles

Actionable Insights:

Take time to think about the elements, people, and experiences in your life that read like poetry. Create a list that captures these moments of joy and inspiration. From your list, identify what truly matters to you. These are the verses that compose the soundtrack of your life. Make a conscious effort to prioritize and nurture them. When you engage with these 'poems' in your life, immerse yourself fully in the experience. Be present and appreciate the emotions they evoke.

Poetry is everywhere and is relatable to every element in our lives. *Think! Because it's all interconnected.*

THE POWER OF UNWRAPPING THE PRESENT

We look back and it is a river of memories of our lives,

Memories from such moments, which changed us forever,

Which brought us little closer to each other,

Which split us farther from each other.

Weren't those seconds the ones we lived the most?

Which make us want to go back to it?

<u>*Quote says:*</u>

We often try to save the present for the future instead of living in the present. We often look back and feel good that we made memories. Making memories is okay but reliving only in them is not okay. We need to feel and experience so that it becomes the best experience than a memory. Some memories bring us closer to people and the rest take us far away.

Pop Your Bubbles

Picture this: You play a song, and you recall from your memory what to play next. Similarly, you are on a trip, and you want to go to the next destination as quick as possible. **This is not living in the present but living in the imaginations.** Likewise, we tend to get stuck in the past, in some memories and run behind to recreate the good ones and run away to get rid of the rude ones. **In this back & forth life of memories and dreams, how do you think we live in the present?**

As we move through life, we sometimes transform like a butterfly, leaving behind the cocoon of our past selves. Our scars, like permanent tattoos on our skin, bear witness to the battles we have fought. A flower you touch, and caress emits its fragrance, and you want to go back to it. Like a butterfly leaves its skin shades to you, some scars leave marks forever. You tend to carry these highly influential moments forward in your life.

But here is the twist: time, like a one-way road, does not allow U-turns. You cannot revisit those moments; they are locked away in the vault of memories. **Is it possible to go back to memories?** Even if you get back it is again only in your memories. Physics proposes that time is irreversible. Then why do you still dream of a day that is already gone? What is the point of living when all we do is live in memories? Recalling memories helps with emotional balance and valuing days and people, but what about the new memories that we are missing out on creating/experiencing? What if these new memories are going to be better than the old ones?

Just that we live in memories more than the present moment. Read that again. We live in imaginations than the present. We want to get back wherever we have felt the most alive. **Are we running back to those memories because they offer a taste of life we miss?** Since we feel memories are a better place for us to live, to feel alive and safe. Are not memories - because they feel lively, the reason for us to go back to it? So that we live it a little more for a little longer? Because we did not live fully that day, in that moment. Isn't present a present (gift) we did not accept?

Actionable Insights: The next time you find yourself lost in the loop of nostalgia or daydreaming about a future yet to come, take a deep breath. Ground yourself in the present moment. Observe the world around you, the sensations in your body, and the people you are with. Remember, the present is a gift. Unwrap it, cherish it, and make it a memory worth revisiting in the future. *Think! Because it's all interconnected.*

MESSAGES TO "POP YOUR BUBBLES"

Perception Questioners	138
How to Understand People	140
People Pleaser	142
Feeling offended by People	144
Feeling Disappointed	145
Insecure People	147
Lonely People	149
Self-Centered People	152
Jealous People	153
Follow your Heart	157
What is the Meaning of Life	158
Wanting to be Extra-Ordinary	159
Seeking Happiness	161
Mother's Love is the right definition of love	165
Trauma Healing	166
Pretending Wise	168
Be My Forever	169
Death is Painful	169
I don't have a passion	170
Create a Lasting Impact	171

➜ A Message to Pop the "Perception Questioners" Bubble

Life is like driving a car; we can only see the road ahead, but we understand it better when we look in the rearview mirror. These past experiences, dear reader, become the brushstrokes of our perception. As Soren Kierkegaard once wisely mused, **"Life can only be understood backwards; but it must be lived forwards."** Our perceptions are the brushstrokes that paint the canvas of our understanding. Just as a skilled artist transforms a blank surface into a mesmerizing masterpiece, so too do our life experiences shape the way we perceive the world. **But what exactly is perception?**

As the great Albert Einstein once mused, **"Reality is merely an illusion, albeit a very persistent one."** Perceptions, my dear friends, are like the seasoning of life. They add flavor and depth to our understanding of the world. Imagine being in a room filled with a hundred people. Each person holds a unique puzzle piece, and they are all trying to complete the same picture, each with their own idea of how it should look. Negotiating in such a room can be a head-scratcher. Just imagine the peace in the world with so many non-negotiable perceptions. That is when rules & order come into play, wherein a human is forced to perceive with filter of the rules, for the peace to sustain. So that everyone is on a common ground and shall perceive from the right direction. **Rules are everywhere, in our home, temple, self, & life.** If not, there is only chaos to prevail.

Those rules are the virtues of life. Without a common ground rule and reality, how can a perception be in a life-enhancing direction? If humility and honesty are not important life virtues, then even stealing and killing people would not be crimes. That is the importance of knowing, understanding, and abiding by the base rules. Perceptions are parts of the complete truth with which we experience the world based on our virtues and experiences, those are bits and pieces of life. Agree? Then what is the use of perceptions if it is not the ultimate truth or reality? **Perceptions are the lessons that mature into the truth.** The main difference between the truth and perceptions is that the truth cannot have perceptions; if **"a book is on the table,"** which is the truth; how else can it be perceived? For instance, it can also be perceived as **"the table is under the book"** but there should be a rule involved to perceive in the right direction otherwise everything in the world has perceptions equal or more than the count of people existing to perceive it. For the book and the table here, the rule would be **"Where is the book?"** now **"the book is on the table"** is the perception in the correct direction. If you think that the book can be perceived from different directions, like **"the book in the hall,"** **"the book is in my home"** etc. then the rules to perceive in this way are different too. **Perceptions are samples of truths that mature into a single truth, and that is why it is important to perceive in the right direction.** This might be a simple example popping such a complex bubble, but life can be understood only by simple thoughts because I've understood that **life is simple, in real too, it's complex just in our minds like a bubble.**

Amidst all this perceiving, have you ever paused to think about the truth? As Mahatma Gandhi once said, **"Truth never damages a cause that is just."** How can something as fundamental as truth be seen in a billion diverse ways? Truth, my friends, is universal and steadfast. It does not change, and it certainly does not put on disguises. **It is the same for everyone, just like the fact "Sun rises in the east" is.**

Perceptions, you see, are like the filtered snapshots of your life experiences. They are not the truth itself; they are more like opinions people form along the way. As Marcus Aurelius wisely stated, **"Everything we hear is an opinion, not a fact. Everything we see is a perspective, not the truth."** Then where do we find the truth?" The truth, my dear readers, is a bit of an enigma. It can only be experienced and felt, it is injustice to even describe it by words as it becomes a perception because language itself is a filter or perception. As Rumi beautifully expressed, **"Do not be satisfied with the stories that come before you. Unfold your own myth."** Keep seeking in the right direction and the truth will find you. So, as you navigate the world with your unique perceptions, always remember to seek the truth within, for it is in those moments of pure experience that you will find the most profound wisdom.

➜ A Message to Pop the "How to understand people" Bubble

To comprehend others, we must first comprehend ourselves. Like a mirror reflecting our inner truths, self-awareness becomes our guiding light. Even after we understand and listen to people we are surprised and puzzled by some unpredictable parts of them. Everyone here wears a safety mask and that is the person we see and know. The actual human is beyond the mask and the filters. Wouldn't it be great if we knew that part of them?

Humanity shares a set of unspoken rules that define our interactions. Discovering and respecting these rules are the first steps towards understanding others. While we are all unique individuals, we share a common desire for peace. Beyond the shared ground, lie the desires, values, and emotions that shape our lives. Emotions are the threads that weave the tapestry of our lives. Understanding their influence is the key to decoding human behavior.

In essence, we can know people in 2 ways:

- **Knowing, observing & being aware of self: the mirror of self:**

Humans are similar yet different. Similarity is that we all seek peace and difference is that the definition of peace is different for you and me. **That is why knowing yourself helps you understand the similarities between people.** The more you know yourself, the more you will understand and know others. Once you know yourself, when someone is not like you, you are able to spot the difference. Because it's always that we know others through ourselves. The similarities are like the ground rules of any human. When you know the rules, you can figure out the path to their differences very subjectively. Because every one's ground rules look like being honest, loyal, love, hate, care, help, offer, give, take. To abide by these rules' humans, commit subjective deeds, hence everyone unique. For example, I desire to give (ground rule) all lot to the Universe, my way of giving is via this book which gives me happiness (ground rule), becoming entitled is the last thing I expect. Perhaps, to you giving is helping poor or needy.

Understanding the ground rules will eventually help you be better at knowing and understanding people.

- **"How you do anything, is how you do everything else!"**:

Once the ground rules are set and understood, there are other facts about humans' needs like desires, money, wishes, victory, care, love etc. these can be understood by how they navigate through daily life. How you do anything, is how you do everything else is true with humans because we navigate via the base values and experiences, we adhere. Any decision we take is dependent on the base values we have. There is an emotion attached to everything we do; may it be known or and underlying unknown feeling. But these feelings and values in combination work the mind map in relation with life and people. Since everything is attached to an emotion, however you do anything is how you do everything else. **It is a pattern in the mind and works irrespective of the situations.**

How you maintain your living space is how you accumulate your thoughts. If daily cleanliness is maintained, that means you organize your thoughts and have good clarity. If the living space is messy and cleaned once it is full, it means that you decide to organize only when you are overwhelmed.

Even in the little decisions in life, like picking a dish from the menu at a restaurant in between a regular food item and a new food item, a person who picks up novel items is ready to try new things and is not hindered by insecurity about losing. A person who picks the regular food item is in their comfort zone and is not inclined to take up new opportunities unless they are convincing or are something they have had partial experience with in the past.

The list is huge; perhaps you'll read it in my next book. This is a skill that I developed, through observation and self-awareness. It is easy to navigate life, if you are able to understand people. Most of you are stuck and insecure because you do not understand people. **Life is always with people, all of us have to deal with people.** You can't escape people. Understanding people quickly has made my life better. Our quest to understand people is a lifelong adventure. By honing our observational skills and deepening our self-awareness, we illuminate the path to richer, more meaningful connections.

→ A Message to Pop the "People Pleaser" Bubble

In a world where the desire for inclusion, approval, and validation often drives us to please others, it is crucial to understand the hidden costs of this behavior. We often bend over backward to please others, discover how to reclaim your authenticity. People-pleasing often finds its roots in our early experiences, where we learned that conforming to other's expectations was a way to gain acceptance and avoid rejection. If you felt neglected by parents, or if they did not validate your actions and desires, you may carry that longing for validation into adulthood. The struggle to create and maintain friendships during our formative years can also lead to people-pleasing, as we seek to satisfy our innate desire for companionship.

People-pleasing is not a one-size-fits-all behavior. Some individuals become extreme pleasers, while others engage in it sporadically. It manifests when we say "YES" instead of "NO" to please others, when we prioritize their needs over our own, and when we do things solely to win favor.

Have you gone through the following circumstances? If yes, you are or have been a people pleaser too:

- You tend to say a "YES" while you wanted to say a "NO"
- You tend to prioritize others instead of yourself.
- You tend to do stuff for people when asked for help, not out of love, but to want them to like you.
- You deliberately help even when you are not asked, not for they needed it, but because helping them will make you useful for them.
- You tend to be exactly like what they want you to be like.

- You vouch for them, even when you know it is not right or you do not believe in it.

Beneath the surface, people-pleasers grapple with inner turmoil. By consistently denying our true desires and suppressing our inner voice, we accumulate frustration and anger. This suppressed rage can manifest in physical ailments and psychological issues. The more we choke our true selves to gain the approval of others, the more negativity surrounds us.

Continuous denial of our authentic selves can lead to a growing gap between who we are and who we portray to others. This disconnect deepens with each act of people-pleasing. The draining nature of trying to please everyone further depletes our energy, as every act requires us to silence our inner voice and pretend to be something we are not.

The solution lies in embracing our true selves. Remember that nobody is inherently good or bad; everyone is trying hard to fulfill their desires and voyaging through their life. **Be yourself means, do what your inner calling tells you to do.** If you want to say a "yes," say "yes" instead of a "no." Start off with small steps, if someone has asked you to lend money, do not promptly say a YES, ask time instead, say **"I'll think about it"** and later if it does not feel right to you, deny being helpful. Take baby steps because we have been pleasing people from years and immediately just after reading this, you cannot change. Go mellow. Change will happen. If you do not want to go for that hangout, opt out. If you do not like her outfit, do not appreciate but do not depreciate as well. Just do what your inner voice pushes you to do, instead of pleasing others. If someone asks for a favor, take a moment to consider before responding. Gradual change is the key; you have been people-pleasing for years, so be patient with yourself. Opt out of events that do not align with your desires and maintain honesty without hurting others. **Remember, the hidden costs of people-pleasing are high, but the rewards of authenticity are immeasurable.**

➔ A Message to Pop the "Feeling Offended by People" Bubble

We feel offended when our insecurities are poked. The root of feeling offended is in our ego which tries to protect and hide our insecurities but when triggered the ego is immediately thrashed and there is huge offense. To tackle with feeling offended we need to heal from insecurities.

Feeling secure is like the most naturally need in the world; it is practically hardwired into our very beings. But when you are not feeling secure, that's when things get a little rocky.

"Insecurity is like a little scuff, but it's the one thing that connects all life on Earth. We all want to feel safe and secure."

Even the tiniest creatures on this planet, from the ants scurrying around to the mighty beasts roaming the wilderness, they all share this deep-seated desire for safety and security. It is in our DNA, passed down from our ancestors who had to learn some tough lessons about survival.

We are offended not because they intentionally tried to poke you but because you gave them the power to do so. They got the power because you don't have control of yourself. The key is to feel secure in oneself by accepting our insecurities. The moment we resolve our insecurities internally, we feel beautiful about the same flaw which we once felt offended about. Imagine your friend triggering your strengths, doesn't that feel like an appreciation to you? Perhaps say your friend calls you an excellent dancer, which you are. Then you are on cloud nine, enjoying feeling appreciated. This is because you accept that you are an amazing dancer and believe in it. Same is to be done with the insecurities to convert them into admiration and appreciation.

Pop Your Bubbles

➔ A Message to Pop the "Feeling Disappointed" Bubble

Disappointment is like a distant relative of hurt. It is the first step on the journey into those hurtful emotions we all know so well. Imagine it as the opening act, where the curtains rise on the stage of emotional turmoil. How deep it goes into the realm of hurt depends on the size of the emotional wave it rides. When the effect of hurt is less, we feel disappointed and when the effect is large, it is hurtful. This happens when the effect is other than what we expect.

But here is the thing – it all starts when life throws us a curveball, something unexpected. We humans have this funny habit of creating little mental blueprints of how things should be, even for the tiniest stuff. When life does not conform to our mental diagrams, we are left with a sense of disappointment. Now, here is the burning question: What can we actually control in this whole experience? Well, it is the part where we can simply stop building those towering expectations in our minds and gracefully accept whatever life serves us.

Let us switch gears for a moment and talk about people. We meet them, we think we know them, but here is the truth – You can never fully unravel the mystery of another human being. Let me break it down for you.

As you interact with people, you start to sketch patterns of their behavior in your mind. You connect the dots, constructing intricate portraits of who you think they are. From the trivial, like predicting if your friend will pick up the phone, to guessing their culinary preferences at your favorite Chinese restaurant. You become experts at deciphering their behavioral codes.

But here is the twist – people change, constantly. The person who was a music aficionado yesterday might be the star of a dance floor tomorrow. Your beach-phobic friend could be catching sunrise at the shoreline, and the one who had your back through thick and thin might switch sides. **People are like a box of assorted chocolates; you never really know what flavor you will get.**

So, what is the deal, you ask? You are navigating a world as unpredictable as a game of dice, often overlooking the beauty right before your eyes. People are as unpredictable as life itself because they are, quite literally, life in action. They change, they evolve, they heal, they throw you curveballs, and they learn. **It is a continuous evolution, and here is the kicker – you cannot ever fully "know" them; you can only learn about them.**

Instead of trying to fit people into neat, predictable boxes, let yourself go with the flow. Embrace the surprises, both delightful and not-so-delightful. Treat people like strangers, even if you have known them for ages. Imagine meeting a fresh version of them every day. Picture it: Each day is an opportunity to learn and grow without the sting of disappointment or the boredom of predictability.

So, drop the habit of creating those mental blueprints. Next time someone asks if you know what someone is going to do, just say, "I don't know." Because, honestly, you do not. You sometimes pretend, and sometimes you guess right, but other times, you are off. The truth is, nobody can predict someone else's moves except for the person themselves, and most of the time not even themselves.

Let's embrace people as they come, without building walls in your mind. Those walls belong in their heads. By embracing, I mean accepting the fact that people change, and you cannot expect anything from anyone. People are like surprises delivered by Mother Nature herself, and she is one unpredictable lady. People are part of nature, but they sometimes forget to let it flow naturally. And resisting that flow? Well, that will not do any good.

➜ A Message to Pop the "Insecure People" Bubble

Feeling secure is the innate need of humans, it is the intelligence of human nature. Insecure is feeling not secure from within. Feeling insecure looks a minor scuff to talk about but every life on earth from the tiniest ant till the giant animals, everyone wants to feel safe and secure. It is an innate need and has evolved from our ancestors based on the survival of the fittest. Early days, when the need to eat was unmet and ancestor humans like the neanderthal, sapiens etc. could not locate food, they used to eat each-other. They used to eat based on the survival of the fittest where any human who was unfit to be useful any further in their group, was chewed off. That is when people started to contribute largest outwards to the group and keep truly little for them. **That is when people started feeling insecure about themselves, about their worth, their value, their contribution, their existence.** That is when safety for living was not guaranteed. This passed on through generations and it took a lot of forms and patterns and in this world where we have everything available, at least the plight that we need to kill each other for food is not there.

Earlier lack of food created insecurity and now, excess of amenities is doing it. Instead of dropping insecurities, we created more of it, by showing the lack of the excess in everyone. Insecurity has taken new forms; it has become more about self-lack than that of food or other factors. It is feeling insecure about life and invalidation.

If we investigate insecurities deeply, its base is fear and mostly is fear of missing out (FOMO). People have created norms and rules on how to exist and how to be, once we are away from such norms, people invalidate us, trigger all the negative emotions in us, pass all the insecure comments & make us feel low about ourselves. We then hate ourselves in our own skin. We begin to strive hard to feel secure and accepted in the society. We tend to change ourselves which people can accept. That is how insecurity looks on the outside but there is so much else to this.

This is how insecurities deceive others into controlling you. Insecurities are not about feeling invalidated, triggered, or low by the world but by invalidating yourselves. You know that there are norms and rules which will help you be in the world, but choosing to accept oneself the way you are is important. You will not feel invalidated by the world only if you validate yourselves. You will not feel triggered by the world, only if you accept yourselves in your own skin. If you have a darker skin-tone, you need to accept your skin tone first, only then the world will. **Who created the norm of fair skin is beautiful?** God created every one of us, and God has not said I will not love the dark-skinned humans. Every shade is beautiful in its own sense. Same goes with thin body type vs fat ones. It is all in your mind, if you accept the way you are, no one can trigger any part of you. If you accept yourselves, the world will automatically do.

We should look at humans as you look at the flowers, when you look at some flowers with five petals and then look at a different flower with three petals, you accept it, you do not say it should have five petals only then it is a flower of beauty. We humans make each other's life difficult; this is a message to all the judgmental eyes to not judge and to all the insecure people to not judge.

There are two types of insecurities, one is external and internal. External occurs due to external invalidations. These include insecurities around looks, outfit, body, skin, money, status, familial status, etc. Is there any end to this list? Absolutely not, this keeps going on as a never-ending list. And you keep acquiring all these to feel secure. While the list is never-ending, this will keep increasing over the years, can there be any end to external insecurities? You will acquire some more money to feel secure, then you will acquire some more money to feel secure, because this is a never-ending loop. Only acceptance is the key here, you need to accept that this will suffice your needs and that rushing behind money will get you nowhere, hence, just letting it go with the flow will help. Similarly, accepting your looks, shade, complexions, body shape will end your insecurities. **Security begins when you accept your insecurities.**

The next is **internal** insecurities; this is related to feeling the lack of love, care, loneliness, weakness, inabilities, etc. all these feelings of lack of these emotions can be completely fulfilled by no one except you. **You need to back yourselves up.** You need to be there for yourselves. Do not seek these emotions from outside or from other people, this will only create more such voids, because people change, people are unpredictable, people are bizarre. Only you are consistent with yourself, make sure you fulfill yourself and admit to self-care.

➔ A Message to Pop the "Lonely People" Bubble

Loneliness is not just an emotion; it is an ever-present companion in our lives, wearing different masks like solitude or aloneness. These friendly disguises of loneliness hold the key to finding inner peace, and to discover it, we must first embrace feeling lonely.

Imagine loneliness knocking gently on your door. What do you typically do? You might rush to escape it by calling a friend, burying yourself in chores, or diving into a binge-watching session. Doesn't loneliness look like a trigger for any action? Remarkably, scientific studies have shown that it ignites the same brain regions as hunger. Now, we know why some people are big foodies. As hunger is a cue to eat, loneliness is also just a cue. But here is the revelation: It is not lack of something or emptiness. Loneliness is not a chasm of emptiness waiting to devour us. Deep down, we are inherently social beings, wired to connect with others. We are all social animals, and we have our social needs, to interact with humans and connect. Loneliness is just a call to the social needs. Body's gentle nudge, reminding us to nurture our social needs, like a signal rather than a declaration of inadequacy.

In the words of Maya Angelou, **"Diversity makes for a rich tapestry, and we must understand that all the threads are equal in value, no matter their color."** Similarly, all our emotions, including loneliness, are threads in the rich tapestry of life, each with its unique significance.

So, that red flag around loneliness? There is no need to sound the alarm. Instead, let us interpret it as our body's gentle reminder, whispering, "Hey, we need some social energy here!" But here is the secret sauce: do not always rush to answer that call. Instead, practice the art of simply listening to it without immediate action. Let loneliness ebb and flow, much like the waves on the shoreline.

With time and practice, something truly magical unfolds. Those cues that once felt unpleasant transform into something pleasant. Loneliness itself starts to metamorphose into solitude. It is all about rewiring your emotional response and being in your control, turning triggers into soothing sensations, and embracing the beautiful mosaic of human emotions.

In the words of Rumi, **"Don't grieve. Anything you lose comes round in another form."** Loneliness, my friend, can also transform into a form of connection—with yourself and with the world around you. So, let us embark on this journey of self-discovery, where loneliness is not an adversary but a friend guiding us toward the richness of solitude.

➔ A Message to Pop the "Self-centered People" Bubble

For everyone self-love is our guiding star. It is the force that propels us forward, the beacon that illuminates our path. But just like any powerful force, it must be harnessed wisely, for too much self-love can lead us down a treacherous path – the path of self-centeredness, where the center of every situation for us, is us. Any group decision we participate in, we want the decision to be favor of ourselves. Our ego swells and we want everything about ourselves. Self-centeredness is when you do not care about the worldly existence. Being self-centered might feel like prioritizing self, self-love etc. But when there is a major need and a collaborative call, if we only choose what we want, it is being selfish. Most of us are self-centered in the name of self-love. **A lot of myths are attached related to these in our minds.** Self-love never meant not caring about others or not sacrificing our needs for others sometimes. It always meant about being there for our inner child. I read somewhere, **"Try to keep others happy, without losing yours' and try to keep yourself happy without harming others'. "**

Pop Your Bubbles

Imagine self-love as the sun in our personal solar system. It radiates warmth and light, allowing our decisions to orbit around it. Yet, when self-love becomes all-consuming, we risk eclipsing the needs and feelings of those around us.

"Happiness is not a goal; it is a by-product," once said Eleanor Roosevelt. And indeed, true self-love does not mean isolating ourselves from the world. It is about self-care, healing, finding inner peace, nurturing emotional intelligence, and offering a comforting embrace to our inner child. It never meant forsaking others or ignoring their needs; it is about finding harmony within us.

But when we tread the path of self-centeredness, we lose touch with the world around us. It may seem like we are prioritizing self-love, but in reality, we're inching towards selfishness, driven by myths we've internalized. If we are self-centered, we will tend to be unreal in our commitment to others and also in being there for them without a whole heart. There will be no human involvement in it or human connection. **We will not be able to "give" ourselves.** By giving it once, we get it twice or more in return. When we give, a part of it stays with you as well. "I have found that, among its other benefits, giving liberates the soul of the giver," beautifully expressed Maya Angelou. As giving is an innate nature in humans, we will be cutting ourselves off from experiencing it. **We would be stopping ourselves from living the human experience.** While we do so, we disconnect from ourselves more. We can be there for ourselves, but we should make sure we do not deprive ourselves of connecting, feeling, and reciprocating the human experience. Genuine giving is a fundamental human trait, and when we cut ourselves off from it, we miss out on a vital part of the human experience. We disconnect from ourselves even further. So, how do we find our way back to balance? We begin with small steps, mindful of the need to give as much as we receive. Consciously practice acts of kindness, making someone happy each day. Engage in social activities, and when the situation calls for it, put others first. **Change is gradual, and it starts with our commitment to shift our perspective.**

Remember, allowing ourselves to experience the beauty of giving not only deepens our connections with others but also enriches our own lives in ways we could never have imagined. Join social activities. Try to prioritize others when needed. We will change slowly, by committing to the change. Only if we allow ourselves to feel the emotion of giving, we will feel life and live enormously. In the end, it is about embracing the full spectrum of the human experience, both as givers and as recipients.

→ A Message to Pop the "Jealous People" Bubble

Deep within each of us, there is a fiery dragon known as jealousy, waiting to rear its head when we witness others possessing what we desire. This emotion has been our companion since childhood when we were taught to strive for excellence and outshine the rest. As Maya Angelou aptly said, **"Jealousy in the air tonight, I could tell, I will never understand that, but oh well."** This is where our perilous dance with comparison begins.

As Oscar Wilde once quipped, **"Be yourself; everyone else is already taken."** Imagine that every human being is like a unique product on the shelves of life, each carrying its own label of experiences. We must learn to love and accept ourselves as we are and extend this grace to others. After all, no two products are identical, and that's what makes the world so wonderfully diverse.

Picture trying to compare a Starbucks coffee to a sleek laptop - it is like comparing apples and oranges, right? Just as products vary, so do humans. There is no fair way to stack us up against each other because our life experiences are as unique as fingerprints. As Albert Einstein aptly put it, **"Everybody is a genius. But if you judge a fish by its ability to climb a tree, it will live its whole life believing that it is stupid."** Let us bid farewell to this futile game of comparisons.

Transform Jealousy into Admiration. When the green-eyed monster of jealousy stirs within, do not let it consume you. Instead, replace those envious thoughts with admiration for the person who ignited them. Challenge yourself to learn from them, to grow, and to become more like the person who sparked that jealousy. As Coco

Pop Your Bubbles

Chanel wisely noted, "**I don't care what you think about me. I don't think about you at all.**" Jealousy, my friend, is actually a marvelous teacher in disguise.

Envision a fish gazing up at a bird soaring through the sky, feeling envious of its ability to fly. **Now, picture the bird gazing down at the fish, envious of its graceful underwater dance**. The irony here is clear: both possess unique strengths and capabilities. So, why waste time on jealousy when we can celebrate our own exceptional talents? The irony here, if the fish is jealous of the bird's flying, the bird is jealous of the underwaters.' Perhaps, you are jealous thinking your friend could ace the event and your friend is jealous that you got enjoy the event back in the seat, peacefully. **It is an unwanted loop**. Eliminate it.

➔ A Message to Pop the "Follow your heart" Bubble

Two distinct groups of individuals emerge over the years, as people grow. The **first** is ablaze with an insatiable passion, their hearts dancing with dreams and desires. The **second** group, however, appears to have misplaced their passion, or perhaps it's been hidden away. To the world, they might seem identical, but within, they sense a profound difference.

For those filled with passion, a curious dilemma often unfolds. Society whispers in their ears, urging them to relegate their dreams to hobbies and allow their jobs to sustain them. Humans, naturally social creatures, crave inclusion in the mosaic of existence, whether amid the hustle and bustle of a city or the tranquility of the countryside. Over time, society has painted a portrait of 'acceptable' and 'prestigious' professions, casting a shadow over our passions. As we venture to follow our hearts, a storm of "No's" pours down upon us. These negations plant seeds of self-doubt, causing us to question the validity of our passions. **Insecurity creeps in, and our beloved dreams suffocate within.**

Amidst this turbulence, one unwavering truth persists - our belief in ourselves. We tend to doubt our ability to pursue our passion, but we will never question our ability. The love for our passions runs so deep that we inherently know we can pursue them. It is as if we stand at the threshold of possibility, keys to our dreams just within reach. We mistakenly believe these keys lie in the world's hands. In truth, they have always been firmly grasped in our own. A single leap can unlock the door. Visualize the This urge will and can-do wonders, I swear. **Once the door is unlocked, the bird who had just realized about the presence of its wings, will begin to fly forever.**

Can you visualize it? Your dream, your passion as a reality beyond the door, isn't it coercing to unlock it? The urge to unlock it can work wonders, I promise. Once that door swings open, you become a bird discovering its wings for the first time, ready to soar endlessly.

Imagine a life where you clutch your passion close while enduring a stifling job. Imagine doing a job while we breathe on our suffocation passion every moment. A dreadful day is always better than a bad life. It is that we are deeply condition by the society that we second guess our moves. **If you believe it, do it. Initially it will be a tough ride, later, when you excel in yourself and your passion, people will accept and respect all the choices you made.** Society's expectations have been etched deep within us, leading us to second-guess our every move. But if you believe in your passion, pursue it. Initially, it may be a tumultuous journey, but as you excel, people will not only accept your choices but also admire and respect them.

Consider this story: A shoemaker whose father, has passed away, and his son now holds the position of CEO in a prominent company. During a conversation with a friend who serves as a director in another firm, the CEO is playfully taunted, "Don't forget, you and your father used to visit my home to mend my shoes." The CEO responds gracefully, "Indeed, my father was an exceptional shoemaker. He poured his heart and soul into his craft. While I may not be the best CEO, he was undoubtedly the best shoemaker, and his art is still remembered." Contemplate the profound difference in perspectives.

Pop Your Bubbles

Always remember, there is a marked contrast between work executed with passion and dedication and work done solely for a paycheck. When love and passion guide you, every endeavor transcends mediocrity. No achievement surpasses the splendor of work executed with love.

Frequently, the roles society assigns us are transactional and devoid of soul, completed merely to meet deadlines and earn a living. Yet, work should be an outpouring of love. **You often mistakenly believe that money is the key to happiness, falling into the trap of such roles.** You barely realize that while we work with heart in it, it gives us reward of joy and happiness without money. Passion should also be detached; you call it a passion because we are emotionally into it which influences our decisions on a larger scale.

Passion, you see, should be a detached emotion. We label it as such because emotions serve as a huge driving force behind our decisions on a major scale. As Albert Einstein once said, **"I have no special talents. I am only passionately curious."**

For those who have yet to uncover their passion or find themselves bound to jobs solely for financial or life circumstances, do not despair. **Alter your perspective on your work.** Infuse small droplets of affection into your daily tasks and witness the transformation of your perception of the job.

Emotions in relevance with passion - Once upon a time, I was caught in the grip of low spirits, all because I had come to define myself solely as a writer. My emotions were bound to this identity, and I can admit that I had moments when the number of likes and comments on my work functioned as my daily dose of dopamine. However, when triggered by criticism, whether online or from anyone around me, I would spiral into a vortex of overthinking, leaving me drained and distressed. It was as if I had poured my very soul into my writings, my blogs, and the art of storytelling. Consequently, any critique, no matter how well-intentioned, felt like a personal assault.

It was during these moments of introspection that I realized a transformation was necessary. I needed to shift my entire perspective on my passion for writing. So, I took a step back and detached myself from my writing. This seemingly simple act led to something profound. Criticism ceased to be an attack; it became valuable advice. Comments were no longer about me but rather reflections of the commentators. **Offences lost their personal sting.** Every word I wrote became a drop in the ocean of change I wished to bring to the world, no longer a plea for likes and validation.

You see, every artist retreats into a secret realm of creativity, a space far removed from the harsh realities of life. It is a sanctuary where we can weave our stories, paint our pictures, and compose our music. To truly explore and create, we must detach ourselves from the world outside and our passion to some extent. **Having a passion is still like having a relationship with it, so detachment is equally important for a long-term vision.**

Consider this: If someone labels you as a good public speaker, several scenarios might be at play. You might indeed be an exceptional speaker, or perhaps the person appreciating your skills lacks a deep understanding of public speaking, making you seem extraordinary by comparison. Alternatively, you might relish the praise despite feeling somewhat inadequate as a speaker. That is perfectly okay. You take that label and use it as motivation to become the excellent public speaker you are now known as.

We are all guilty of embracing the labels others place upon us. We begin to define ourselves through their perspectives, carrying these labels as if they were precious gems. Eventually, we merge these labels with our very identity. **When criticism comes our way, it feels like an assault on our very essence.** We scramble to defend these identities, fearing that we will lose ourselves if they are taken away.

But here is the revelation: It is all because we identify ourselves with these labels. **We attach ourselves to these identities, as if they are the heroes of our stories** and when that hero is threatened, it feels like the end of the world.

But here is the twist: The true hero of our story is not the writer, the public speaker, or any label we have adopted. It is just us, stripped of labels, entitlements, and identities. **It is about recognizing that our core identity is not tied to what we do or how others see us.**

Once you embrace this truth, all the defensive actions you take to protect our identities from criticism become unnecessary. You find neutrality, and we make peace with yourself. The story goes on, and the hero within us shines brighter than ever, unburdened by the weight of labels and identities.

→ A Message to Pop the "What is the meaning of life?" Bubble

Life is a journey of personal meaning. In the joyous play of existence, life and time are intertwined, much like actors on a stage. Life, on its own, is like an empty canvas, and time is like a ceaseless river flowing. But here is the captivating twist: We humans are the artists who splash colors onto this canvas, and the captains who navigate the river of time. **Without us, life and time would be monochrome and aimless.**

Think for a moment, what if life had a fixed, universal meaning, like the word "happy" that carries the same definition for everyone? It would be a mundane existence, wouldn't it? Life, however, is anything but mundane. As the great playwright William Shakespeare once wrote**, "All the world's a stage, and all the men and women merely players."**

You see, life is as diverse as ice cream flavors, and our experiences shape our preferences. It is unique for each of us because we explore, learn, and, most importantly, imbue it with our own flavors of significance. To quote Albert Einstein, **"Imagination is more important than knowledge."** So, why do we persistently seek a one-size-fits-all meaning? It is akin to chasing the elusive end of a rainbow, believing there is a pot of gold awaiting us.

Even in our relationships, we crave meaning. We yearn to be more than mere footnotes in someone else's life story. We are like master chefs in life's kitchen, combining ingredients to craft a unique masterpiece. But here is a secret worth, cherishing life is not a frantic sprint; it is not a contest to outpace others. It is a leisurely journey, akin to a road trip with no predetermined destination. To echo Buddha's wisdom, **"The trouble is, you think you have time."** You are the author of your life's narrative, and each day offers a fresh page to fill.

So, my friend, take a deep breath and let go of the relentless quest for a universal purpose. Life is a thesaurus and humans are its meaning, likewise humans are a thesaurus, and we create our meanings. Just live it.

➔ A Message to Pop the "Wanting to be Extraordinary" Bubble

Do you ever notice how everyone seems to be on a quest to become extraordinary? It is as if we are all chasing after a shimmering mirage that keeps moving farther away, like chasing our own tails. But what if I told you there is a hidden gem right here in the ordinary, waiting to be uncovered?

As Albert Einstein once wisely said, **"There are two ways to live: you can live as if nothing is a miracle; you can live as if everything is a miracle."** In our relentless pursuit of the extraordinary, we often overlook the wonders that surround us daily. Let us embark on a journey to rediscover the extraordinary within the ordinary.

Picture this: A friend once asked a wise saint, "What's the secret behind your remarkable peace and wisdom?" The saint's answer was disarmingly simple: **"There's no secret at all. I eat when I eat, sleep when I sleep, walk when I walk, and feel when I feel."**

Now, it might sound deceptively easy, but it is far from it. This philosophy involves taming the wild monkey mind, mastering our emotions, cultivating self-awareness, and nurturing our inquisitive spirit. It is about taking the reins and guiding our minds, rather than letting our minds run amok. Often, as we eat, our minds wander off into the past or the future, rendering us physically present but mentally absent.

But here is the beautiful paradox: Being ordinary can be the most extraordinary thing of all. Henry David Thoreau once wisely remarked, **"It's not what you look at, that matters, it's what you see."** Embracing the present moment, fully engaging with the simple act of eating or sleeping, is a remarkable achievement. It is the foundation upon which everything else falls into place.

→ A Message to Pop the "Seeking Happiness" Bubble

In the quest for happiness, have you ever found yourself chasing after fleeting pleasures? Picture this: Life's experiences are like a magnificent orchestra, each instrument playing its unique melody. As the great Viktor Frankl once wisely remarked, **"Happiness cannot be pursued; it must ensue."** Just as different instruments create a symphony, our life experiences craft our unique pursuit of happiness.

We form our experiences and pains of different genres create unique voids in us that match the pain. Our different voids seek fulfillment. We try to fulfil these with temporary forms of happiness. Sports might make you happy, but movies might make your friends happy. But do you see what is common here? We seek them again and again because the craving arose again or was not satisfied then. We all want to be happy, so we seek sources of happiness. We all want permanent happiness, which is the state of bliss, but we seek temporary sources of happiness like sports, movies, smoking, money, sex (pleasure), travel, etc. The thing about happiness is that it is a state of being, not a phase. These temporary stuffs give us pleasure because they are temporary, while happiness is a state of being that cannot be squeezed out of anything. If you can enjoy a comfort zone, a piece of music, a form of literature, or an art form, there is pleasure in it. We do not get pleasure from the inside; we are getting pleasure from the inside. Pleasure is a dependent emotion that will not sustain itself. It is a short-lived high. We get pleasure and feel happy.

In our pursuit of happiness, we often resemble the butterfly flitting from flower to flower, each offering momentary nectar but never truly satisfying its hunger.

But here is the thing: **Happiness is not a fleeting phase; it is a state of being.** Happiness is always with us; we tend to ignore its presence. You know you can simply sit and be happy, randomly watch a kind gesture and become joyous than the counterparties involved. You can just be happy. It needs you to just be involved with heart. It is that feeling of complete engagement with the present moment, where work becomes play, and time loses its grip. Imagine happiness as a deep, serene river, undisturbed by the chaos on its surface. It flows from within, irrespective of external turmoil. Yet, as we chase momentary pleasures, the finish line seems to recede further away with every step. Our indulgence in these fleeting joys only magnifies the void within. Like a marathon where the finish line keeps moving away, the more we seek these pleasures, the further we feel from lasting contentment.

To experience true happiness, you must let go of the need for external triggers. It is about achieving a state of bliss where appreciation and criticism merely exist as reflections of other's perceptions and sometimes, a simple change in our actions can lead to a genuine shift in our emotions. By acting happy – adopting the right posture, words, and actions – we can induce happiness from within.

As Mahatma Gandhi wisely noted, **"Happiness is when what you think, what you say, and what you do are in harmony."**

Sometimes, just acting happy, can make us happy. Research says action and emotions are interconnected. If we act happy or sad, we can bring in those emotions. By acting happy, means we need to use appropriate posture, talks, words, actions. If we are emotionally happy, our actions will align automatically. If happy or sad emotion, can bring about relevant actions then happy actions will bring in happy emotions. So, next time you are stuck in traffic, rather than venting frustration, hum your favorite tune. By acting wholeheartedly, you can transform a stressful situation into a moment of personal joy. In this journey from acting happy to being happy, we unlock the transformative power within ourselves, moving beyond the shadows of fleeting pleasures toward the radiant light of lasting happiness. There have been cases where the movie actors get so involved in that scene, that they live that emotion, be it sorrow, happiness, depression etc.

If someone appreciates you for your looks, speech, material commodity, behavior etc. immediately we feel pleasures and happiness and inflate our ego. If someone criticizes you, you will be hurt, not because they said wrong about you, but because your ego is hurt. This is how triggers look.

To be happy, you must be in a state of bliss. Nothing should trigger happiness; it just is. It is when you feel constrained within. A satisfactory sense of being. **It is not a triggered state of being.** If you see the wide sea, it is calm. It is in a state of calmness, and nothing triggered it to be so. Even if there is a fire accident, a forest fire, or any calamity, it just stays calm irrespective of those. Likewise, with us, we will be in a state of bliss when there are no triggers for our happiness or sadness. The appreciations and criticisms will not trigger, and we just observe them as a source of their perception. Be aware.

➔ A Message to Pop the "Mother's Love is the right definition of love" Bubble

Once upon a time, in the world of boundless love, there was a mother. She embraced her child with warmth, showered love like rain, and shared the wisdom of life with her little one. This, my friend, was a love so pure and real that it touched the hearts of all who witnessed it.

But let us dig deeper into this notion of a mother's love as the ultimate form of love. Imagine your mom as the superhero of your life. She is always there, ready to save the day, teach you the ropes, and be your unwavering supporter. A mother does caress, love, teach and is selflessly bringing up her kid. For her, her child is the best source of love and is everything. She can give and do anything in the world for her kid. **All this can be the best form of love we see in real life, but mother's love is not the right definition or correct form of love**

rather it is just the best form of love that everyone has felt. Since, your mom always cares, shows up, has your back, teaches you, is dedicated to you, sacrificing her needs, you feel that it is the best form, henceforth, you compare and contrast with the universal love. Her nature makes you feel good and her deed towards you makes her feel good that she owns or possesses you. Of course, mothers love is meant to be dedicative and sacrificing but commenting it as the best form is irrelevant. **"A mother's love is like no other,"** we often say. Yet can we say with certainty that it is the pinnacle of love, the gold standard, the one to beat?

Consider this scenario: Your mom's incredible, right? But how does she treat your friends? She might be mom-like to them, but with you, she is a full-fledged mother. Perhaps, to an extent she would be motherly but later all her decisions will be more inclined to your safety and growth. This is somewhere intentionally selfish and not the purest form of love. It is not just love; there is a dash of self-interest there. **"Motherhood is the essence of selflessness,"** some say, but it is not pure altruism; it is a bit like comparing apples to oranges.

Love, my friend, takes on many forms. There's mother's love, sister's love, brother's love, and countless more. **Some say that a mother's love is the best, but that does not mean it is the purest.** When you add a father's love into the mix, as parents, they raise their kids. Yet is not it curious how many folks out there seem troubled, dealing with traumas, depression, anxiety, and sometimes even despair, despite having those noble parents? If mothers love is the best in your experience, it does not mean that there is nothing better than a mothers love as love. **Definitely, there is a purer and more selfless form of love.** No offense to mothers out here, of course mother's love is beautiful, and I am sure you are doing your level best.

Here is an analogy: Your parents are like architects, designing the foundation of your life. Sometimes, they use the best materials, and other times, they unknowingly create cracks in the structure. It is not always intentional, but it is the impact of their own experiences shaping your world.

Pop Your Bubbles

If love can heal anything in the world and mothers love is the right form of love, why is everyone who are raised by those noble parents still suffering from traumas, depression, anxiety, suicides etc.? A mother does not raise the child, she just grows a part of her body, in her own way. She fulfills all her dreams and desires through her kid, because she thinks that since she gave birth to the child, the child will fulfill all those dreams because it is liable to her. She tries to project all her traumas onto the kid so as get rid of her traumas. An infant child is the most innocent being on the earth and she puts all her thoughts, dreams, ideas, traumas, wishes onto the kid, so that the kid feels is immobile, helpless and cannot express itself. This is definitely intentional, but that is how her mother has the possession towards her kid.

"Motherhood: where dreams meet reality," they say. Being able to bring a child into the world is a remarkable gift from nature, no doubt. But once that child is born, they should be allowed to explore, express, and love themselves. Imagine using an AK47 to squash a tiny ant when a gentle tap would do the trick. That is a bit like the way we overload newborns with our own ideas and rules, inadvertently crushing their sense of self. They stop feeling themselves before they start understanding 1+1 = 2. Their focus turns away from expressing, talking, exploring, asking to just fulfill your thoughts because they are made to feel liable.

Now, do not get me wrong; a mother's love is indeed a beautiful thing. She is a giver, constantly dedicated, caring, and willing to make sacrifices for her child. **But sometimes, it is not just about her love for the child—it is about how it fulfills something within her.** She gets dedicating as a mother because she is also able to express the motherly side of her. When she talks about her child, it is not always about the child; it is often about her, too. **"A mother's love knows no bounds, but sometimes it seeks its own reflection,"** goes the old saying. "My child is good at art," she says, but it is not just about the child's talent; it is about her role in it. "My kid loves football," she claims, but it is not just the child's love; it is her sense of accomplishment. And when she says, "My kid can't do this," she is not just stating a fact; she is making decisions for her child, sometimes without even realizing it. But here is the real kicker: **If a mother's love were truly the pinnacle of noble love, then every child she raised would be living happily ever after, right?** Well, that is not always the case.

Here is a fable: Once, there was a king who owned a magnificent palace. He treasured it, kept it spotless, and took immense pride in it. But when fire accident and his palace was under attack, he left it behind without hesitation, running out with his family. His son was puzzled by his father's actions and asked why he did not seem to care about the burning palace. The king simply replied, **"It was not mine. I sold it last year."**

So, my friend, perhaps love, especially a mother's love, should be a state of being, not something tied to ownership. Why should a mother only love her child because they are biologically connected? Why can't she extend that love to the neighbor's child? **"Love begins in the heart, not in the blood,"** they say. It is this idea of possessiveness that often leads to suffering in the world.

As the saying goes, charity begins at home. And love, well, it should not be about extracting love from each other. Before a mother gives birth, she should heal from her past traumas and mental issues. There should be some sort of qualification or preparation before becoming a parent, including therapy to ensure parents are emotionally ready. After all, everything we do as parents has a profound impact on our children. As charity begins from home, everything else begins from home. **Love is not extracting love from each other.**

Before a mother gives birth, she should be healed of her past traumas and mental issues. There should be a degree with passing marks for eligibility to be a parent. The parents should attend therapy sessions and heal themselves because trauma is the last thing any newborn would cherish as legacy from his parents. **Everything impacts the kid at a larger extent than it should.**

So, my dear reader, let us raise our children, not just grow them. Let us love them, not demand it. Let us let them be themselves, free to express, explore, and follow their dreams, not just ours. In the end, love should be a journey of self-discovery, both for the giver and the receiver, a beautiful symphony of hearts, not a possession or a burden.

A kid should be raised, not grown.

A kid should be loved, not asked of it.

A kid should feel himself, not fear self.

A kid should express fully, not devoid of it.

A kid should fulfill his dreams, not his parents.'

➜ A Message to Pop the "Trauma Healing" Bubble

As the great psychologist Carl Jung once said, **"The meeting of two personalities is like the contact of two chemical substances: if there is any reaction, both are transformed."** Life often delivers these transformative moments when we least expect them, and we label them as "trauma." But let us shift our perspective. Traumas are not always negative; they are the catalysts of personal growth.

Recall the happiest memory in your life. Mostly, it was an unexpected moment, a delightful surprise. These are the **"Happy traumas"** that etch themselves into our hearts. On the other side, the painful experiences also linger, resurfacing when you least anticipate them in the name of traumatic experience. In life traumas are normal because life is unpredictable. It is just that you create a scary notion around traumas. While you allow happy traumas, why cannot you allow the sad ones. It is our interpretation that can cast them in a negative light. While we readily embrace happy traumas, we tend to avoid the sad ones. Yet, resistance only magnifies their impact. **"What has happened has happened,"** as Shakespeare wisely noted. The moment we resist trauma, it tries to bounce back with a higher force. Viktor E. Frankl, noted that **"When we are no longer able to change a situation, we are challenged to change ourselves."**

Traumas are emotional wounds. Just as you care for physical wounds with tenderness, emotional wounds deserve the same care. Initiate an emotional surgery to facilitate healing. Start by accepting the emotional wound in your mind, ensuring that your body does not resist recovery.

Begin with emotional cleansing. Let the pain flow, release it, and do not be afraid to shed tears if necessary. As author Rumi aptly put it, **"The wound is the place where the light enters you."** Once you have purged the emotional turmoil, give yourself the gift of time. Engage in practices like meditation and mindfulness. Use daily affirmations, as Louise Hay advocated, to reinforce positivity.

Over time, view subsequent triggers as mere memories and let them pass, much like clouds in the sky. When those painful memories resurface, consider them as mere echoes from the past, and let them pass. Remember, healing emotional wounds is a profound journey. It begins with accepting that traumas, both joyful and painful, are integral to the unpredictable mosaic of life. Embrace them, cleanse them, and allow yourself to heal. It is through these experiences that you grow, transform, and ultimately become resilient souls.

➔ A Message to Pop the "Pretending Wise" Bubble

The vast ocean of information that envelops our world, I once found myself adrift, tangled in the relentless pursuit of proving my wisdom. It was not just about validation; it was about the immense pressure I placed on my own shoulders to highlight my intellect. I was driven by an insatiable hunger for knowledge, determined to become a walking encyclopedia. And there, looming over me, was the notorious FOMO, the fear of missing out.

As I navigated through the ceaseless waves of data, it became abundantly clear that the growth and expansion of knowledge in every field were both unstoppable and inevitable. Countless streams of information flowed and evolved at a pace that felt almost surreal. But in this overwhelming torrent, could one realistically keep up with the

Pop Your Bubbles

constant stream of updates from a million different directions? Moreover, what was considered hot and trending in one part of the world might barely register as a blip on the radar in another. Hot topics, I soon realized, changed faster than we could utter the word "trending." Most of all hot topics keep changing in fractions of seconds. A topic which is hot today, may not be hot tomorrow. Overall, the same topic is not talk of the day for more than a few days to months. How does all this prove me wise?

So, a question gnawed at my soul: **Does this ceaseless chase truly make us wiser?** Does it substantively prove anything? After all, the information we so casually exchanged in our daily conversations was just a few keystrokes away on Google. It seemed almost foolish to regurgitate facts that were a mere click away. In essence, were I not imposing unnecessary pressure on myself? In this case, **I would only win if I became a walking google.**

True wisdom, my friend, does not lie in the parroting of facts but emerges from the crucible of experience. It stems from a deep understanding that transcends the scope of Google's vast database. While Google is undoubtedly a convenient resource, it primarily deals in the realm of the general and readily accessible.

However, the real jewel lies in discerning the authenticity of the information that crosses our path. It is in the ability to sift through the noise, separate fact from fiction, and distill genuine knowledge from the vast sea of data.

But wisdom? Ah, that is an entirely different tapestry. It is the art of self-awareness, the proficiency in navigating the intricate labyrinth of life. It is about understanding the depths of your own mind, gaining dominion over your thoughts, and plumbing the profound depths of your own being. How do you think? How do you truly know yourself? These are the questions that underpin all meaningful values.

Have you ever encountered someone who not only answers your questions but also lightens the burdens of your life's journey? They do not merely impart knowledge; they illuminate your path, making your voyage through life less daunting. Trust me, it is a blessing to really feel and be wise, make peoples' lives lighter. I have been there, on repeated advice diarrhea when request. I have made sure I cast the impact they need, to push themselves out of any life loop. My heart yearns to say this, **"Wisdom is gained from daily conversations with oneself, not others."** To quote the wise philosopher Lao Tzu, "Knowing others is intelligence; knowing yourself is true wisdom. Mastering others is strength; mastering yourself is true power." That, my friend, is the treasure we should fervently seek.

As I reflect upon this journey, I realize that true wisdom is not about proving oneself to the world, but about understanding and mastering the world within. It is not about the endless pursuit of external knowledge, but the deep exploration of the self. And in that quest, we find the true essence of wisdom - the power to not only know, but to transform our own lives.

➔ A Message to Pop the "Be my Forever" Bubble

Are you or I meant to stay together forever? Well, as the great Maya Angelou wisely put it, **'Some people come into your life for a reason, a season, or a lifetime.'** We are here for a limited time, and that is just the way life goes. But why is it that we often yearn for everlasting connections, even when everything around us is in constant flux?

Life itself unfolds in phases, each with its distinct timeframe, much like the changing seasons, each bringing its unique beauty and purpose. As someone once said**, "To everything, there is a season, and a time to every purpose under heaven."**

Consider relationships, my friend, they are a lot like the world's seasons. Some relationships bloom and wither quickly, like the ephemeral beauty of a wildflower. Others, however, stand tall and sturdy, much like the steadfast oak tree.

People enter our lives, much like characters in a narrative, and each carries a unique role to play. But, like actors exiting the stage once their part is done, these individuals leave our lives just as mysteriously as they arrived.

Yet, here is what makes this journey truly captivating: Not every encounter is meant to be a timeless masterpiece. Some, like pieces of a puzzle, come into our lives to help us see the bigger picture. They arrive to reveal what is right and what is wrong, to inspire us to become the best versions of ourselves, or simply to provide a comforting presence on those moonlit walks where we spill our deepest thoughts.

➔ A Message to Pop the "Death is Painful" Bubble

In the grand symphony of life, you are but notes, born from the same melody as the leaves, the mountains, and the rivers, just as the great philosopher Albert Camus once pondered. As nature is born from the womb of your Mother Earth, you are born from the womb of your mother who is already nature. You are all just nature, before humans. As everything else ends, death is your end as well. **And just as the sun sets, one day, you return to her loving embrace in death.**

Picture a humble plant in this vast garden of existence, a silent but wise teacher. It stands its ground, unwavering, for it knows that fleeing would only lead to an endless chase by the storm. It tries to survive all the storm & if it stays, it stays. It accepts anything which happens to it. It does not run away from it. If the plant ran away from it, the storm would follow. Nobody rejoices or rejects it presence. But still the plant lives fully and lively. It is happy being unnoticed, unvalued, unrewarded because it does not have emotions. It also dies after it reaches a certain stage. **Why? Because it lacks the emotions that drive us.**

As Eckhart Tolle eloquently points out, **"We humans crave validation, yearn for attention, and seek rewards. It is our conditioning; the mold society has shaped us in."** The key to our freedom lies in breaking free from this conditioning, like unlocking a treasure chest buried deep within us.

Our purpose is a simple one - to live our lives. Our birth, a gift from the divine, a trust we call **'Amanat'** in Hindi. It is akin to God saying, **'I trust you not to squander the life I've bestowed upon you.'** This trust is a sacred responsibility that we must honor.

Now, what if I told you that pain has a purpose? It is the teacher that guides us to learn and grow to live life better. So, when you are told that pain is good, it is not to make us endure suffering needlessly, but to remind us that even in our darkest moments, there is a lesson, an opportunity for transformation. Instead of shying away from pain, you can embrace it as part of the intricate, beautiful story of our lives, a story authored by nature itself."

This revised version maintains the core message while enhancing clarity, engagement, and overall flow.

➔ A Message to Pop the "I don't have a Passion" Bubble

Everyone was non-passionate in the first place, some people clicked with some passion, the rest are still exploring, and it is okay!

I have met people worried about not having a passion or a goal. It is okay, life is a journey without a destiny, you are living it right. If you have a passion, you have a direction in life and you can find meaning in it because you are enthusiastic about something and that is it. If you do not have a passion, you have ample paths to explore multiple opportunities to take charge on, you can find meaning in exploration and live through it, why can't exploration be a passion? It is always the non-passionate person who explores more because he is not horse eyed. It is always the passionate person who becomes an expert and an example to the rest of the people & even for the non-passionate ones. It is a mix and the world need more of both, with an established balance.

→ A Message to Pop the "Create a Lasting Impact" Bubble

Why do you have to create an impact before we leave the world? Why not do it while you are alive. Creating something big so that it lasts forever is okay. But creating an impact before you die is like creating an impact good or bad, so that you do not have to face its aftereffects. Isn't it cowardice? Why exist later in life, after one hundred more years, nobody will remember what you contributed. If you want to create an impact create it now, while you are alive, so that you can witness it and answer the questions it has before you leave the world. Create now and let it last forever if it can.

Thought Provoking Thoughts

- Do not discuss your goals while you are at its start, discuss while you are in the middle of seeing it real. While you are half done, you won't to be pulled down by all the jealousy, demotivation, and the societal noise.
- Happiness does not change us whilst pain does because we want happiness.
- Any experience devoid of the good chemicals in our body causes change in us. We fear, worry, sick around pain while it is a state of devoid of the chemicals. If we change a bit, the chemicals will be back. But why do we think that change is hard, it is just a chemical trigger.
- What we do not find in our homes, we look for them outside. But instead, we need to look inside. Be it emotional or physical.
- Look at people as people, avoid looking up or down on them.
- Anyone can know something you do not know. Every person out here is amazing and has jargons to impress. Imagine X years of learning and later you share the meetings with each other. Do respect.
- Every new label/identity just is making you feel more validated and accepted in the world, do not be proud.
- Any new experience or happening in the world has a label. That label builds a category, and the people belong to that category now feel safe just because of that label.
- We keep longing for higher connections. A married couple are satisfied and share a good connection, when that connection is stable, we want more connection, hence we want kids. This keeps going on.
- You need to still heal from the parts of us, you do not talk about. You have not accepted it yet; hence you still cannot talk about it, its farer from healing although.
- If you fear, you are unhealed.
- You think you do not judge & it is a placebo!

- Watch yourself, how you speak nicely to your boss and rudely with your apartment guard. Drop all this, respect the sensitive & delicate humans. The more you accept the world, the more you will accept the self and vice-versa.
- Avoid keeping strict & tight deadlines in a creative field. With the pressure of the deadline, the bubble of creativity is pressured as well. Add rewards to all the mini goals you get by each step. Helps! For other tasks related to household chores, assignments and tasks which require the least creativity keep the deadlines, strict, tight and abide by it.
- Whenever you want to change, change the way you think about it.
- Stories add value & life to things, stories make life worthwhile. We always look for answers. Because stories help us live.
- You are like chameleons; you take after the corresponding hues of the people and the environment around us. You are not supposed to be so.
- Stop shrinking into places you have already outgrown.
- Excess of anything is worthless.

More Thought-Provoking Thoughts about People

- Choose people who tell you what you need to hear even when it is hard.
- Notice efforts & consistency of the people, rest is all noise.
- Choose people who celebrate your accomplishments as if they were their own.
- Choose people who will back you up, in your absence.
- Choose people who will call your name, in a room full of opportunities.
- If you are a giver, remember to have limits because takers do not have any.

- We only want freedom from what we enjoyed once. Like if you love pizza, try having a 100, just because you love them. I bet; you'll hate it.
- We want to escape what we rejoiced once. The toys we played with in our childhood are in the trash already. Call it a need of change instead of a need for freedom. Things will fall in place.
- We mostly talk to save our identity. See closely when you feel offended. You try to protect your identity, strongly. When I got comments on my passion for writing at the start in my ninth grade. I used to try and protect it, despite of knowing that I might be wrong here. It is a human urge to protect self.
- Higher energy influences us, and lower energy is influenced by us.
- When two people meet, the one who has higher energy will impact the other person. This is the case with any interaction. Even on my blogs, the blogs in which I had maximum energy invested in, that impacted a lot of people.
- Do not take anything personally.
- Whatever people say it is more about them than about you.
- Any face will instantly become beautiful when it is decorated with a smile.
- Be a pro at saying "NO" and bad at saying "NOT." "NO, I do not want to hang out with you. You cannot do this; it is NOT in your scope."
- Every flaw is good, perhaps an attention seeker can be a good host.
- Until we do not accept our flaws, they are insecurities, once we do, they add to our beauty.
- Learn acceptance.
- See through a naked mind.
- Do not judge them, the less you do, the freer you become.
- When you give, you return. Call the science of KARMA. When do we give, we return to the Universe? When we get, someone else returns to the Universe.
- We need to surprise ourselves as much as life surprises us.

Pop Your Bubbles

- Be curious, be explorative, be like a kid.
- The more awareness and self-consciousness you practice, it becomes involuntary, like you breathe. Like we set a habit, we start exercising only a daily basis with cues like alarms etc. Then our body takes the alert automatically and urges you. Likewise, awareness becomes a habit eventually and it is the best habit to instill.
- People see where you come from, do not pose. The people will feel your intentions. That is what energies convey. It will be felt before even you utter a word. Hence, do not pose as if you care or do not care. Do not fake love. Do not pose.
- Nothing will make sense until we organize it mind. Mind can record data but makes conclusion on those only when we organize them.
- It is a never ending now and here.
- We tend to give what we expect. The saddest people always try to make people happy, because they know what it is like to feel worthless, and they do not want anyone else to feel the same.
- Beginnings are happy or sad, endings are always sad, but the journey makes worth the ends.
- Life is beautiful because it has no destination, no rules and is unpredictable. We are suffering this.
- We are always ready to share stuffs or our darkest secrets anonymously. That is where we are attached to our identities and cannot let them go.
- I wish friends after teenage continued to say more of "Love you" and held hands, like we as kids always did.
- Wonder how our growth made us uneasy there.
- A friend to all, is a friend to none. He will compromise your friendship for the other in dilemmic situations for his own benefit.
- When you gift a flower, a little part of the flower's fragrance always stays within you.
- When you are a giver, some part of that giving will always reside in the name of happiness within you.

- When you love an open book, you better love it between the lines.
- Love involves dedication.
- We can only shatter and fall back in front of the people who you know can pick and stick us back together.
- We choose our behavior based on how the people are.
- Celebrate privacy, keep phenomenal secrets between you and yourself. You will regret opening up to everyone.
- As we add value to time, we add value to our experiences via our emotions as well.
- We make our time useful or useless. We emotionally invest in our experiences. That is how experiences change us.
- We tend to give parts of ourselves to the people, who take it along with them and later we keep looking for our lost part in others.
- If you cannot invest in relationship, do not build them. It will create voids for you.
- When there is fear, it is either just in the mind or because of the past traumas.
- Body and mind keeps count of our experiences. Body gets scared. I recently met with an accident and now I stun in fear even in the daylight. Heal.
- Do not love, out of fear of being alone or of losing someone.
- If you love someone, be prepared to let them free.
- Do not fall in love, be in love, live and grow in love.

HOW TO KNOW SELF?

Ask questions thinking you are on a first date with yourself. Be curious and keep adding a chain of questions to get a deeper understanding. Example, if you like to cook, which part cooking excites you and why? It is a time, energy and focus taking process but with patience, you can do it. Observe yourself, talk to yourself, be self-conscious. Be where you are, think in whys' & what's.

1) Do you know why is it important to know yourself?

Only when you know yourself, you get to understand why you are the way you are. The more you know about your depths, you can improvise on what you need to work on – it's like spot the error to fix. Also, as you know yourself more – your understanding about people, grows. As it's like the **"SPOT 10 DIFFERENCES BETWEEN TO SIMILAR IMAGES"** which we've played on paper. It makes living life a lot easier.

(Even if you still didn't get it, trust me and try)

2) Define yourself in a line?

Try to talk about yourself in one line every now and then. It says nothing about who you are but hugely about how you see yourself and what are your priorities.

3) What do you identify with?

What is your region, locality, star signs, religion, school, college etc. Any word which adds to helping in recognize you are the identities you are attached to. While we need them for identification tagging emotions of pride and regrets, are to be thwarted.

4) What are you labels?

The words you use for yourself to hide or show your flaws. These labels mostly come out of self-belief. These beliefs may or may not be true.

Like I'm a good speaker, while you know you are not.

Like I'm a dancer, while you know you aren't.

If you are actually good at it, don't attach it to your identity and find pride out or it, respect your art and respect will come your way.

5) What are your values in life?

Is it compassion, kindness, generosity, self-awareness, helping, care, love, beauty, physical presence etc. Those are the values which you will judge others and yourself with. If there are absurd values try to fix them, because this has got a massive impact in yours and your partners' life too.

6) What are you good at?

There's no end to this list. What are you actually good at which adds value to others life. Take these terms and have it as a cherry on top of you and not an ego bubble.

7) What are your insecurities?

Insecurities are parts of you what you hide. Try to find and observe,

What don't you talk about yourself to others?

Why you are comfortable or uncomfortable talking of that body part of yours?

Insecurities are to be realized because they are majorly involved in making us feel stuck, unhealthy, and unfree.

8) Whom do you look up to?

Pop Your Bubbles

Try to find out what exactly you admire about the person. What intrigues you about it and realize - what you admire is what you want to become.

9) How often are you controlled by your senses?

Check how many times did you snack up, while your tummy was already full. If physically there was not hunger, there was emotional hunger which craved for that snack.

Check how many times you watched that favorite scene from the movie, repeatedly. There was some emotional pleasure which was seeking it and not the visual beauty of the scene in particular.

Check how many times you wanted to feel touched and caressed by someone. Same goes with hearing and smell.

10) How does your comfort zone look and feel like?

What comforts? – makes you feel safe where you are not in a struggle and in a non-alert mode. That's why you don't want to hangout very often and go out to meet a new friend. While comfort zones are cozy, they make us lazy too, spot the thin line.

11) What do you think other people admire about you?

"You are beautiful," "You are smart," "You are a topper" are these most frequent words you've heard from people around you. Those are the compliments you've got because the opposite person is just not as good as you at it. These are the regions what your pressured and seeking perfection about because there is more expectation around it from you.

12) What makes you feel safe?

If you are feeling unsafe, what would you do to safeguard yourself. It may be a person or a space you go to. It may also look like listening to some music. Anything, but find out what made you feel unsafe.

13) What are you careful and considerate about?

Is it money, fame, food, friends, family etc. these are what you will prioritize while you take any decisions. May it be gifting someone or be it hanging out for a while.

14) Which topic brings a rush of happy emotions or bright smile on your face?

Is it writing, football, games, music, reels, cooking etc. that is what is your hobby or passion is.

15) What does relationship/friendship mean to you?

On what grounds would you build this ship. Is it going to be care, support or service. Make sure you realize and communicate it, as it involves a counterpart. There are infinite learnings about self from relationships, focus and observe.

16) How do you see your friends' character?

You know others from how you are not from how they are. See what you think about, it was always about you.

17) What don't you fear, and others do?

Pursuing a degree or going on a solo trip, if you fear it, take baby steps. It will work. Those are the paths you should take in life; they will buy you more confidence and self-worth.

18) How you speak about yourself?

Pop Your Bubbles

Talk about yourself in diverse ways, you'll learn people skills, learn to face rejections, feel authentically connected to people. Talk about your perceptions. A new perception will help you know yourself more. Explore new parts of you. Try to explore places, and it explores parts of you, that you thought never existed.

19) How do you do what you want to do?

Are you attached to the results or the progress? Are you doing out of pressure or desire.

Detach to explore anything, more. Anything you want to learn, if you detach from the "ME" in its process, new horizons will be revealed. Any artist goes into a zone of creativity, which is away from reality, just to bring out the realities. We need to detach from itself to explore itself more.

20) Try meeting new people?

A new person will teach something new about you. It was never who the other person is, it is who are you and that is what meeting people teaching us. Touch all the directions. Talk to people, people push you towards knowing alternate perceptions.

21) How do you talk to people?

Do you listen keenly with involvement or just want to bombard your drama unto them.

22) What do you admire?

People do not admire what they do not have, but what they want to have, you will tend to appreciate others of what you think you lag at.

23) Check how you introduce yourself?

The number of labels you use are your identities and stop them before they become your ego. I used to introduce myself as a writer, but now-a-days people come to know me as a writer, later. This is not getting attached to your identities.

24) Notice what offends you?

You feel mocked or taunted at because you are insecure about that part of yourself, and you do not people to discover your weak points.

25) How do you behave when you are alone?

Your character is when you are alone in a room. When nobody is watching. Spend time with yourself more when you are alone in a room.

26) What short-term/long-term goals do have for yourself?

You can think about many more such questions and get deeply connected with yourself. The more you know yourself, the more you will love yourself and you will feel less lonely.

Bravo! Excellent Job! You Made it!

Reading is not an easy task for all, I know.

*Just wish you to carry forward the messages to **"Pop Your Bubbles"** in your life and cultivate more self-awareness. Good Luck!*

If you're here! I'm sure you enjoyed reading my book, – Consider giving your feedback on **Amazon or Instagram**! It is a **gift** in return to me. Thanks, Cheers Saloni. :)

WHY DON'T SELF-HELP BOOKS WORK NOWADAYS?

The following may also be the reasons why you didn't make the best out of this book.

1. **Mismatched Content:** Not all self-help books will resonate with every reader. The content, style, or approach of a particular book may not align with an individual's personality, needs, or values.

2. **Lack of Action:** Simply reading a self-help book without acting on the advice provided often leads to minimal or no results. Real change requires practical implementation.

3. **Misinterpretation:** Misunderstanding or misinterpreting the book's concepts can hinder its effectiveness. Effective self-help may require guidance or clarification to understand and apply correctly.

4. **Inconsistent Application:** Inconsistency in applying the book's principles can lead to limited success. Effective change often requires ongoing commitment.

5. **Quick Fix Expectations:** Some readers approach self-help books with the expectation of quick fixes or instant transformation, which can lead to disappointment.

6. **Resistance to Change:** Resistance to change, fear of the unknown, or a reluctance to step outside one's comfort zone can limit the effectiveness of self-help efforts.

7. **Overwhelming Choices:** The self-help genre is vast, and it can be overwhelming to choose the right book. This abundance of options can lead to indecision and inaction.

8. **Cynicism and Skepticism:** Some people approach self-help books with skepticism, which can hinder their receptivity to the content.

9. **Incomplete Information:** Self-help books may not cover all the nuances of a particular issue or may not offer a comprehensive solution to a complex problem.

10. **Ineffective Writing:** Some self-help books may be poorly written, making it challenging for readers to engage with or understand the content.

www.ingramcontent.com/pod-product-compliance
Lightning Source LLC
LaVergne TN
LVHW061612070526
838199LV00078B/7254